Master/slave Relations:
Handbook of Theory and Practice

Robert J. Rubel, PhD

Master/slave Relations:
Handbook of Theory and Practice

Published by The Nazca Plains Corporation
Las Vegas, Nevada
2006

ISBN: 1-887895-63-9

Published by

The Nazca Plains Corporation ®
4640 Paradise Rd, Suite 141
Las Vegas, NV 89109-8000

Cover Photo by Corwin
Layout Editor, Blake Stephens

Dedication

This book is dedicated to all of you who have the personal courage to explore this form of *structured relationship*. My hat is off to you. This is a path populated with *unusual people*. This is a path for those who walk down *The Road Not Taken*. This is a path for those who are willing **not** to lead a life of moderation, but **are** willing to challenge some long-held and culture-based assumptions about relationships between consenting adults. This is a path for those who are highly self-directed and who are capable of determining and acting upon their personal vision of their own relationship with their own partner.

Bob Rubel
Austin, Texas
2006

The Road Not Taken

Two roads diverged in a yellow wood,
And sorry I could not travel both
And be one traveler, long I stood
And looked down one as far as I could
To where it bent in the undergrowth;

Then took the other, just as fair,
And having perhaps the better claim
Because it was grassy and wanted wear,
Though as for that the passing there
Had worn them really about the same,

And both that morning equally lay
In leaves no step had trodden black.
Oh, I marked the first for another day!
Yet knowing how way leads on to way
I doubted if I should ever come back.

I shall be telling this with a sigh
Somewhere ages and ages hence:
Two roads diverged in a wood, and I,
I took the one less traveled by,

And that has made all the difference.

Robert Frost

Acknowledgments

A number of Masters have influenced me in profound ways as I have been on my Journey of Mastery. In alphabetical order, those who have had most influence are:

- Master Skip Chasey, a man of peace and calm, spirituality and centeredness, who inspires all who come into his presence.

- Master Bert Cutler, International Master 2003, who exudes sagacity and warmth and knows how to give advice and counsel in ways that it can be accepted and used.

- Master Jim Glass, International Master 2001, who serves as a model for what is possible if you set your goals high enough.

- Master Jack McGeorge, Northeast Master 2005, who is the only Master that I know of who has a more detailed Manual of Protocol than I do.

- Master Steve Sampson, International Master 2000, who puts heart and soul into everything he touches, and in return, is enveloped in love and adoration.

- Sir Stephen Siegel, International Master 2005, who demonstrates so well how one can create one's own Lifestyle – that one can be Leather and run a Victorian Household.

- Master Robert Steele, a Master who needs no titles, a good friend and close counselor who constantly nudges me back onto the Correct Path in life.

- Master (the Good Officer) Wes who – with overarching good spirit and love – thinks deeply and writes eloquently about Things Leather that matter in the world.

- Master Z (Dallas), International Master 2004, whose boundless enthusiasm for life, plus his commitment to the Leather Tribe, serves as a model to those of us he touches.

I certainly acknowledge Brenna, my companion since March 2002, who has been at times my Master, my partner and my lover, and who remains a deep and close friend – we just haven't quite figured out the relationship structure. Thank you for editing this book – among all the others. Thank you for staying with me. You make me a better person, in general, and a better writer, in particular.

Thanks, too, to slave mindi, who lights up any room she enters, and who orders my world so I no longer have to think about it. She has indeed mastered service in the spirit of *sprezzatura* – effortless technique. And she's mastered the art of living with me, no mean feat, that.

Now – a special note of deep gratitude and appreciation for my close friend Jay Wiseman, who in addition to writing the foreword to this book, anguished many hours over the text and made the final content edit. The book has been greatly enhanced by his effort.

Foreword

We live in a time of both great and exciting changes in personal relationships. Given the current cultural freedom to choose the types of relationship structures and agreements that work best specifically for them, more and more people are experimenting with highly alternative relationship structures. For example, we see the prominent rise of gay marriage. We also see more and more consensually non-monogamous married people who are quite happy about their arrangement and whose marriage seems to be at least as stable as those in 100% monogamous marriages. Further, we see more and more people choosing to live in expanded family "group marriage" types of relationships.

While many people choose to enter into newer forms of relationships that offer greater freedom and equality than was true of more traditional relationship formats, others are – to the surprise of many onlookers – willfully, mindfully, and freely choosing to enter into intimate personal relationships that offer them *less* equality and freedom. The people making this choice seem to be completely reasonable, normal, and mentally healthy people, yet they intentionally enter into relationships that offer them less freedom than they otherwise could have. What's going on? Possibly something very important. Possibly something that addresses some very core needs of some people.

It's not a new observation to point out that even in many of the most traditional and conventional intimate personal relationships, there is frequently one "dominant" partner and one "submissive" partner. Sometimes this is expressed in very subtle ways, and sometimes this is expressed in more obvious ways, but it's generally the case that this dominant/submissive aspect to the relationship is relatively implicit.

By contrast, within the BDSM/Leather community, every year more and more couples (and larger intimate personal groups) choose to live in ways in which the dominant/submissive aspect to the relationship is relatively explicit.

Within the community, it's not particularly rare for one person to address a particular other person by a term such as "Master" or "Mistress." One frequently sees people who are wearing collars of leather, metal, or other materials around their neck, with these collars locked into place and the wearer not in possession of a key to that lock.

While the meaning of wearing such a collar is open to discussion, it's frequently the case that the person within said collar consid-ers themselves to be "owned" by another person, to one degree or another, and is more than happy about being considered the "property" of that other person. Indeed, for some people, being "owned" by another person is the deepest and happiest type of intimate personal relationship they can conceive of being in, and both satisfies them much more deeply and contributes to their personal growth more fully than more conventional "equal" rela-tionships can.

People known by terms such as "submissives" or "slaves" are frequently "trained" – sometimes to an elaborate and extensive degree – by someone known by terms such as their "owner" or "trainer" to speak, stand, sit, kneel, and act in certain highly spe-cific and particular ways – sometimes accompanied by physical punishment, willingly and even gratefully accepted, for failure to adequately comply.

People interested in explicitly hierarchal intimate personal rela-tionships are even banding together in groups for socializing and mutual education. Indeed, one organization, called MAsT (Masters And slaves Together), has chapters in many major cities.

Thus, while there has been growing interest in having this type of hierarchal intimate personal relationship, with thousands of new such relationships beginning every year, very little has been written in terms of both the theory and the "how to participate in" what are frequently called Master/slave (M/s) relationships. Into that gap has stepped my friend Robert Rubel, and this very valuable book.

In many ways, this is a time of great pioneering in regards to M/s relationships. Robert does a very good job of outlining the overall landscape of much of this newly discovered territory. He provides the reader with a very good guide to the sometimes confusing terminology associated with M/s relationships. He then goes on to guide the reader through conducting a detailed personal inventory in terms of who they are and what types of relationship they are seeking. Robert provides a good outline of the elements of an M/s relationship, including some very important observations on romantic love.

Robert addresses "household" protocols and how the "leather family" might behave, both toward each other and toward the outside world, including agreements and commitments. He also covers methods for resolving problems in a constructive, mutually respectful manner, and he provides excellent material on communications skills.

The book includes essential information about how to intelligently search for a "master" or "slave" and what to do if you think you might have met one that seems right for you. Issues surrounding negotiation and other aspects of the early stage of an M/s relationship are covered in detail. This is followed by a careful and thoughtful discussion of contracts, collars, and related issues.

Finally, the book concludes with excellent material on maintaining both the relationship and the people within it, and some good basic safety information.

This is an important, thoughtful, and useful book. While it is necessarily written from the point of view of how one particular man goes about it, Robert's experience, thoughtfulness, and "time in grade" regarding being in actual, real-world M/s relationships clearly comes through. This is far from being some unrealistic, unworkable, cyber-fantasy.

Robert's background as a successful business executive shines through, and his approach to running a successful M/s relationship in ways similar to that of how a successful business is run is highly useful. Also, his very high degree of personal integrity and his unfailing concern for the well-being of those under him are beyond obvious. Wannabe cult leaders or others looking to "brainwash" people into following them in a non-thinking way will find no help here. By contrast, those seeking to enter into healthy M/s relationships in the non-dominant role will be very helpfully educated in how to spot malicious, manipulative wannabe "masters" simply because such people, while perhaps superficially charming, will never show anywhere near the genuine concern for the non-dominant's well-being and personal growth that Robert always shows.

As I mentioned, in many ways this book necessarily must be a very personal one, and I'm sure that some readers will not agree with some of Robert's statements and/or with some of his approaches. That's all right. Reasonable minds can differ. That said, his understanding of the fundamental principles and approaches is both realistic and very useful, and both his compassion and his humanity are clear.

This is a very good man, and he's written a very good book. I'm very proud to call him a friend, and I'm very happy to recommend this book as an important, useful, and usable guide to this still largely unexplored, but very important, area of human relationships.

Let the pioneering continue.

Jay Wiseman, JD
Author, "SM 101: A Realistic Introduction"

Master/slave Relations:
Handbook of Theory and Practice

Robert J. Rubel, PhD

Contents

Introduction

"i believe that Masters and slaves are people who are willing to commit themselves to living in a way that is radically different from what our society teaches is right and appropriate. As people who choose to live in consensual Master/slave relationships, we defy some of the beliefs our society holds most dear: the belief that independence is the key to happiness and that the desire to control another person is the heart of abuse. It takes tremendous commitment to follow a path that at best is likely to be misunderstood by those around you."

slave marsha, *Keynote address,*
Southwest Leather Conference, December 5, 2003

Have you ever considered that a modern-day Master/slave relationship closely mirrors a traditional marriage of 100-2000 years ago? Have you ever considered that those who now seek a highly structured pairing may be longing for a marriage model from antiquity? If you will grant me this possibility, then this is a book that updates the way one goes about customizing the design of a 21st century relationship that models a 15th (or 19th or 9th) century marriage – with a few twists.

After all, we're also kinky.

This book is for Masters – and also for their slaves. This book is for established Masters or slaves who are curious about what someone could possibly write on the subject they know so well.

This book is also for those relatively new to the BDSM Lifestyle, who are finding themselves *called* to this form of structured relationship, and also for those who are curious about the M/s Lifestyle and are looking for in-depth information.

When you start exploring Master/slave (M/s) relationships, you start discovering a few truths. First, they are usually considered extremely radical/unusual. Second, they are often held up as the be-all and end-all of BDSM relationship structures. Third, you hear that they usually don't last very long.

Let me land on that last point for a moment. Have you ever wondered why so few Master/slave relationships last a long time? The Good Officer Wes created a list one time (http://www. westom.com/leather/longevity.htm). He observed that some of the more common reasons that relationships fail:

- Boredom
- Mismatch between Master and slave
- Lack of leadership on the Master's part
- Lack of focus on the slave's part
- Laziness
- Breach of trust
- Abuse
- Flavor of the month – endless supply of slaves
- Mistaking extended role-play for reality Mastery/slavery
- Lofty goals with no plans to reach them.

He went on to comment about how to keep M/s relationships healthy. His list included these suggestions:

- Provide a clear relationship structure
- Use protocols
- Acknowledge good service
- Affirm your relationship
- Celebrate successes

This is a nice way to begin this book, for it presents a good capsule summary.

Why Have You Bought This Book?

Want a slave? Have a slave? Those who want a slave, why would you want this? In my experience, it's a lot of work – much of it focusing on YOU as the Master, for it may require you to obtain more skills.

Do you have a *purpose* in reading this book? Are you looking for some answer? What would that be? I only ask so you will know it when you find it – if you find it.

My approach to this field can be summarized in the box, below.

When you don't know what to do, do it slowly.
                                                            Jim Hayhurst, Sr.

Not only do it slowly, but do it *thoroughly.* This book contains a lot of detail; some sections assume that you are pretty well advanced in the BDSM Lifestyle. Let me mention at the outset that I strongly recommend that you read five books as companions to this book.

- Baldwin, Guy. Slavecraft. Los Angeles, CA: Daedalus Publishing Company, 2002.
- Baldwin, Guy. Ties that Bind. Los Angeles, CA: Daedalus Publishing Company, 1993.
- Mager, Robert F., and Peter Pipe. Analyzing Performance Problems or You Really Oughta Wanna. Atlanta, GA: Center for Effective Performance, Inc., 1997.
- Townsend, Larry. Leatherman's Handbook, Los Angeles, CA: L.T. Publications, 2000.

- Rinella, Jack. <u>Becoming a Slave</u>. Chicago, IL: Rinella's Editorial Services, 2005.

Ah, a Word of Warning...

This is a book about "power exchange." Power exchange is the term that describes the condition wherein the submissive exchanges his/her authority to make decisions for the Dominant's agreement to take responsibility for his/her happiness and health.

If your experience with *power exchange* comes from the Internet – if you have not actually had a *power exchange relationship* before – this book probably needs to rest in your bookcase until you've built some real-life experience. Before you venture into the world of Master/slave (M/s) relationships, you may first wish to spend some time learning how to manage a Dominant/submissive (D/s) relationship. Second, real-life M/s unions feel very different from long-distance or Internet relationships.

Part I: Common terms and understandings

First, this material is NOT completely generalizable. In the same way that no two marriages are completely alike, no two approaches to living as a Master/slave couple are completely alike. However, while there are many ways to approach these *structured relationships*, the experiences of those who have gone before – those who actively live this lifestyle – can be instructive.

So, let's start out by using some definations get ourselves on the same page. You don't have to agree with these, just consider them to be *operational definitions* for the purpose of making it through this book; as there are regional differences in Leather protocols, so there are regional differences in the meanings of some terms used in our subculture.

Defining Some Key Terms

This alphabetized list certainly won't include *all* the terms you'll come upon in our Lifestyle – just some of the broader concepts. Now, a person is not likely to be ONLY ONE of the following, but an amalgam of a little bit of *trainer* and a little bit of *Dom* and a little bit of *Master* and a little bit of a *Daddy*. Because each person is a *little bit different,* each person has to make their own path when starting or maintaining a Master/slave relationship.

>   **boy or boi:** Again, turning to Officer Wes: "leather boy – a submissive man wanting a Leather Daddy father fig-ure. The word 'boy' in this sense has nothing to do with biological age. It is a mindset." He goes on to provide his definition of "boy mindset" as: "i want to trust my Daddy a

whole *lot*, but there are certain things that will always be off-limits. There are some limits i will never be willing to negotiate." A "boi" is a female boy.

Daddy: Officer Wes defines a Leather Daddy as: "A dominant man into what's generally considered 'kinky.' Likes being a father figure for his leather play buddy(ies)." A *Daddy* differs from a *Master* in that the Daddy offers a more nurturing and supportive model. A Daddy knows the value of discipline, though at times his soft heart gets the best of him.

Dom or Domme: A dominant person who takes control during specific (often negotiated) periods. That is why D/s relationships are often associated with BDSM (Bondage, Discipline, Sado-masochism) scening (a "scene" is an enounter that may or may not include sexual activity. It can take place in private or in a public BDSM party or club.)

Master (adj): A term often applied to a Leatherman who has earned such respect within the Community that other senior Leathermen refer to this person as Master (regardless of gender). This respect is generally granted after years of selfless contribution to the Leather Community as a whole.

Master (n): A man or woman who exerts near total control over another – often pursuant to a negotiated contract. One current *hot topic* is whether or not a person can be a Master unless he or she has a slave – someone who actually *calls* the person "Master." I'll sidestep that embroilment for the moment, please. The issue, here, is whether the person plays primarily in the world of *authority exchange* rather than in the world of *power exchange*. For our purposes, a Master takes *authority* over another either for a contracted period or permanently (more on this at a later point). A Master is a Dominant who could occasionally bottom to someone else – this could be his own slave. In this sense, the Master is referred to as *versatile.* The Master's primary responsibility is to do everything within his/her power to maximize the potential of his/her slave(s). This involves such things as:

- Maintaining and protecting the trust given to him/her by the slave's submission.

- Being clear about the terms and conditions of the slave's service, including restrictions on the slave's activities and Master's rights to use the slave.

- Ensuring the slave's physical, social, emotional, spiritual, and financial wellbeing.

- Providing whatever training, direction and guidance is necessary to develop the slave to his/her true potential.

- Establishing and maintaining effective lines of communication with the slave.

- Exercising care and sound judgment in the relationship, as the slave's condition and conduct reflects upon the Master and his/her House.

Owner: The term "Owner" is starting to be used to describe a permanent M/s relationship based on a simple exchange of profound vows. The Owner pledges to take care of all of the slave's needs and the slave pledges to obey and to serve his/her Owner. Period. Permanently. No contract.

Protocols: In the military sense – a directed series of steps to be followed in a given situation to create a defined, reproducible result. Protocols are used to create an effective *governance structure* in an M/s relationship.

Rituals: A preferred way doing something. For example, you may have a ritual of having cocktails before dinner in your living room while there is a fire burning in the fireplace. Within that ritual, you may have a dozen *protocols* that concern who sets the fireplace, how the appetizers and cocktails are prepared and served, and how the lights, candles, and music are all set up.

slave: A person who has transferred authority over him/herself to another. (Officer Wes: "The submissive is a volunteer. The slave is not a volunteer." Officer Wes goes on to note that the *slave's mindset* would be as follows: "Once i have gained trust in my Master, i am willing to place anything under his control. Over time, i expect and hope that all limits will be negotiated away."

The slave is expected to understand the terms and conditions of his/her submission and the restrictions placed upon him/her. Generally, the slave's responsibilities include such things as:

- Ensuring complete support for Master and Master's Household, including acting to ensure Master's health and wellbeing.

- Appropriately communicating any change in the slave's physical, mental, spiritual, or financial state.

- Being open and honest with Master, discussing freely any issues, concerns, hopes, or fears.

- Being sensitive to the fact that all his/her actions or inactions reflect upon Master and his House.

- Understanding that the slave's primary purpose is the subjugation of his/her will to serve and to please Master. In that light, success not only depends upon how effectively service is rendered, but also the manner in which that service is rendered.

Structured relationship: A framework of systems or methods of accomplishing tasks that defines the *authority dynamic* of a particular Household.

submissive: A person who gives up personal power to another under certain negotiated terms and conditions. The Good Officer Wes explains: "The submissive has a desire to submit to the direction of another person, which in this community we call the Dominant or Top. Their submission may be quite limited in range. For example, they may only want and desire to release their submission in a limited fashion, for short amounts of time and within tightly confined arenas. This type of submissive will generally carry a long list of rules, boundaries, limits, requirements, etc., which they require the Dominant to agree to prior to engaging their submissive aspect within the relationship."

Trainer: A Dominant who is primarily concerned about teaching *systems* that improve and refine a slave's skill set – such as puppy skills, pony skills or other pet skills.

Leather vs. Not-Leather

Before going any further, I'd like to set the stage for the balance of this book.

In a general way, the current and diverse "BDSM Community" has developed from two major *paths.* At the risk of oversimplifying these origins for the sake of brevity, the "Leather" path is an outgrowth of returning gay GIs from WWII, who often associated with motorcycle gangs in the 1950s and 1960s. They bring *hierarchy, protocol* and *spirituality* to their modern-day practices. The other BDSM path, a path that I'll refer to as "Not-Leather," evolved – at least in part – out of the swinging movement of the 1960s and even earlier. The Leather path has greater focus on obedience, spirituality, service and protocols, whereas the Not-Leather path has its focus on amorous love.

> For a definitive historical discussion of the origins of BDSM both in Europe and in the US, see Robert Bienvenu's doctoral dissertation. (www.americanfetish.net)

I'm mentioning these different paths because they carry some implications in relation to how Masters and slaves get together in this current age. Again, while there are no absolutes, there is a *general tendency* in the Leather community for a slave to petition a Master to be that Master's slave. In some cases, there is a tendency among Leather Masters to see it as their duty/obligation to accept such petitions and to "Master" the person – if the Master deems that person ready to be Mastered.

Again, while there are undoubtedly exceptions in the Not-Leather community, it's been my experience that Doms tend to be looking for submissives for play, and that over time, the D/s relationships sometimes drift into M/s relationships – often with little or no formality.

I'm not proposing that one approach is better than another. I'm only pointing out that there are two quite different starting points: a person petitioning to be a particular Master's slave versus a person seeking a submissive or slave.

Describing Some Relationships: husband/wife; Top/bottom; Dom/submissive; Master/slave; Owner/slave

I'm about to wander into the realm of generalities. At least I let you know.

husband/wife: Generally, both partners have equal power and responsibilities; structured *power exchange* (or *authority exchage*) is not generally included in marital vows. In fact, it is unlikely that the average couple-on-the-street would have the faintest idea what you were talking about if you asked them about the role of power exchange in their marriage. In my personal opinion, this is one reason that marriage is so difficult. (I've been in two: each lasted about 17 years. I'm 61 as I'm writing this.)

Top/bottom: In BDSM play, this describes who is doing what to whom and does not necessarily involve power exchange. It's just a description of the physical action. Usually the Top is the person performing the action, and the bottom is receiving the action. You can be a Top and be flogging someone, or you can be a bottom and enjoy a flogging. You can lead the action from the Top position – you can determine which flogger you use and how hard you flog your bottom – or you can lead the action from the bottom, telling your play partner (acting as the Top) to strike a little harder/softer or a little more to the right or left and to *pay attention to the wrapping, please!!!* Master Skip Chasey refers to Top/bottom play as "about the physical body." Master Steve Sampson thinks of it as "about the sexual self."

Dominant/submissive: For our purposes, this is the first level of relationship that involves *power exchange.* Consensus has it that D/s play is situational or time-limited. Often, D/s play negotiations involve discussions of likes, dislikes, and limits. There is one senior Dom in my community who won't play with a new play partner, even for a scene, unless the partner sits down for a formal scene negotiation leading to a scene-specific contract. In a general sense, D/s is about micromanagement. The submissive is not to do anything that the Dom/me doesn't direct. Master Skip refers to D/s play as "about the mental body." Master Steve looks at this play as about *energy.* Despite the *conventional wisdom* that D/s play is time-limited, I can easily imagine long-lasting relationships that have grown to incorporate **negotiated D/s** into a marriage or marriage-like relationship.

Master/slave: The M/s dynamic is generally considered the most extreme form of relationship. In this relationship, the slave has given Master complete authority over him/herself. Now: a caveat. Leather M/s relationships generally begin with a contract that includes paragraphs describing the scope and limits of the M/s dynamic. By that very act, the M/s dynamic is viewed by some as something less than a total commitment to the concept of M/s. This has given rise to a new relationship category – Owner/slave – discussed in the next section. Above, I've mentioned that D/s often involves *micromanagement*. In M/s, the object is that the slave gets to the point that micromanagement gives way to *macro management*. As the slave learns Master's habits, the slave becomes able to anticipate and move to meet Master's needs. The couple is increasingly blended into one being. Often, the M/s dynamic involves spiritual growth that is not common to relationships involving other power dynamics. Both Master Skip and Master Steve consider Master/slave relationships to be about the spiritual body. I know of a number of long-term marriages that incorporate an M/s structure, though these are quite rare.

"…people who know and follow the path of Mastery or slavery are **called**. They believe they were called to follow a different path than the ones our society prescribes for us."
slave marsha, Keynote address,
Southwest Leather Conference December 5, 2003.

Owner/slave: As Master Jim Glass points out: "With absolute ownership comes absolute responsibility." Over the last year or so, I've begun to notice increasing distinction made between *Master/slave* and *Owner/slave*. My first exposure to the concept occurred when SlaveMaster conducted an "Ownership" presentation at Master Taino's Northeast Master/slave Conference in Washington, D.C. in July, 2005. Since then, I've noticed that the term "Owner" is being applied to a relationship that is **not** based on a negotiated M/s contract. The total "contract" is comprised of the slave's pledge to obey and to serve Master and the Master's pledge to take complete responsibility for the slave (see the example provided in Part VII). That's it. Master simply owns this piece of property and its income producing capacity. The slave exchanges total personal authority for total A-Z protection, care, and emotional security.

Now, we've come to the end of this part of the book, but just so some readers don't feel left out, let me mention that I don't want to get into Trainers and puppies or ponies here. Nor do I want to start engaging discussions of swinging, polyamory or Gorean traditions. Combinations spin out of control too quickly.

So, to refocus – now that we've rolled through some forms of BDSM relationships, a question comes to mind: *What are you looking for?*

- An occasional slave for play or a permanent slave?
- A structured relationship or an amorphous one?
- A monogamous relationship or a polyamorous set of relationships? If poly, are you thinking of including other slaves or other play partners?
- Is your life to be centered on sadomasochism (SM – sadomasochism is sexual pleasure or gratification produced by inflicting pain – sadism – or by receiving pain – masochism) or something else?

Chapter Summary

In this chapter I defined terms so that you will have a common language for understanding the balance of this book. These terms included:

- boy/boi
- Daddy
- Dom/Domme
- Master – both as an adjective and as a noun

- Owner
- Protocols
- Rituals
- slave
- Structured relationship
- submissive
- Trainer

I described some relationships:

- Husband/wife
- Top/bottom
- Dom/submissive
- Master/slave
- Owner/slave

That's all we need to cover right now. Next, we'll start in on some self-examination before moving on to relationship issues.

Part II: Self-Examination

What is your *purpose* in entering into a Master/slave relationship? I like Master Jack McGeorge's statement of purpose: To achieve "an enduring relationship between a Master and slave who are worthy of each other." Master Jack goes on to comment that the assumption, here, is that the relationship would last more than two years. He also goes on to define "worthy" as: "Someone whose contribution to your life is commensurate with your efforts on their behalf; someone you are proud to call your Master or your slave; someone who strives to excel in their role." (Master Jack McGeorge's Handout for presentation at Southwest Leather Conference 2005: *Finding a Worthy Master or slave.*)

This rasies the question: how do you find such a person – either Master or slave? THAT answer, to a large extent, centers on how clearly you can confront yourself about yourself and on how objectively you can evaluate the person you're considering as a Master or slave.

Who Are You?

What interpersonal, technical and life skills do you bring to the table?

Before I begin this section, a comment: I've heard people say that they've had (let us say) five years of experience at some skill, yet when you observe them at that skill, they don't appear to be very good at it. From this, I've learned to distinguish between someone who has had one year of experience that they repeated five times versus someone who has had five years of progressive experience leading to skill or knowledge mastery. I further draw the conclusion that some people are dead-set to learn little or nothing from life's experiences and will go out of their way to do so.

So, here are some tough questions – tough, in large part because few people spend the time to think them through before starting a new relationship or maintaining the one they're in. Starting right now and lasting throughout this book, I'm going to be putting forth questions designed to cause you to stop and think. And act. When possible, I'll provide tips and techniques and nudges, but you MAY have to seek out experts and courses to build your

---

"Few people think more than two or three times a year. I have made an international reputation for myself by thinking once or twice a week."

G.B. Shaw

"Thinking is the hardest work there is, which is probably the reason why so few people engage in it."

Henry Ford

---

strength in certain fields.

A Guide to Thinking:

- Think more slowly.
- Don't limit yourself to two alternatives.
- Don't confuse hindsight for insight.
- Think on paper.
- Don't set out to prove yourself right.
- Do learn from mistakes.
- Ask questions.

What are your skills and personality assessment scores?

I'm an educational sociologist by training, but spent my career in business settings. My slave is an RN-paralegal. We are used to working differently. When we first came together as a Family there were some stress points. Given a task to look something up, my slave worked any problem to DEATH and created a paper trail of EVERYTHING done – reams of copies of Internet findings, for example. In an effort to figure out how to approach her and how best to use her ample skills, I put us through a battery of tests. So, I pass this tip on to you: use some objective measures to figure out how YOU work and how your partner or prospective partner works.

- What's are the Meyers-Briggs scores for you and your partner? Have you studied how <u>your</u> type gets along with <u>his/her</u> type? (Hint: the personality test offered on alt.com is essentially a Meyers-Briggs and it enables you to compare YOUR test against any other member of alt.com. If you and your slave take their test, the resulting analysis and compatibility discussions can give you a good starting point.)

- How do you take in (process) information? There are a number of ways that you can think about the way you learn. One of the most common ways of cutting this topic describes three basic modalities in which we convert information to memory: visual (learning by seeing), auditory (learning by hearing), and kinesthetic (learning by doing). Most people use one predominant modality, but some use a balance between two or even all three. As it relates to M/s relations, not only must you be in touch with the way YOU learn, but also be sensitive to the ways your current or potential slave learns.

- What are your preferred *working styles*? Are you mostly a *fact finder* or are you mostly good at *follow through*? Are you a *quick start* or are you better as an *implementor*? We found that the Kolbe A test (http://www.kolbe.com) was the single best test to reveal how each of us worked as individuals and what we had to know (and do) to improve our abilities to work together. Yes, there is a modest cost. YES, it's worth it.

A true story. The person who introduced me to Neuro-Linguistic Programming (NLP – the folks who have mastered *learning modalities*) commented that until he understood about this process, he would get furious at his wife for coming up behind him and putting her hands on his shoulders while he was reading at his desk. He later came to understand that she was a kinesthetic learner and was expressing her love for him through touch. He, though, was a high-visual learner who would get completely absorbed in reading. The act of being touched at that time not only broke his concentration, but also broke his emotional state – he didn't like to be touched.

There are many ways of understanding how you and/or your partner understand things. For more information about learning styles, try a Google search on "learning modalities."

Been married?

- How did that work out? Are you still friends with your husband/wife? Is there more than one ex? Were there similar problems with each marriage? Are you carrying problems from one mate to the next? How could you change to make this new relationship different from prior relationships? Without changing yourself, have you ever considered that *this is as good as it gets?*

- What's causing the breakups? Have you spent time thinking about what went wrong? Have you had help thinking this through – been through some therapy? If yes, can you express what you learned and how you changed? If not, what makes you think you won't repeat the patterns you went through before?

- Did you nurture your prior spouse or partner? Can you explain how they grew under your care – either as the Dominant or submissive in the relationship? Did YOU do all the growing? Did THEY do all the growing?

- What will you do *this time* that will be different?
What have you learned over the years? Remember
Einstein's comment: the definition of insanity is "doing
the same thing over and over again and expecting different results."

How's your work history?

- Do you have a history that demonstrates stability or
transience?

- Do you have a history of working well with small groups
and with your peers over a long period? If not, what
makes you think you can lead a slave?

- Have you had special training in managing people?
Do you read body language easily? How are you on
picking up non-verbal cues?

- Are you a visionary or an implementor? Think about
that one: if you're an *implementor* at work, how do you
become a *visionary leader* in your M/s relationship?

Do you have "leadership power?"

- Are you able to get tough when the situation demands
it?

- Are you able fully to show your human qualities instead
of wearing a mask?

- Do you have a clear vision for your future?

- Do you share your vision with the people who follow
you – bringing them enthusiasm, high energy and con-
viction?

- In a work setting, when subordinates ask for directions
or decisions, are you able to direct and decide without
delay?

What do You Seek?

At the risk of proposing polor extremes, consider some of these:

- Do you seek a servant to follow all your orders and whims or do you seek a cherished partner who expresses love through service?

- Do you seek a live-in sex object or do you seek a spiritual partner with whom you have hot sex?

- Do you seek an invisible chef and maid or a personal assistant with privileges?

Hazy goals produce hazy results. Clearly define your goals. Write them down, make a plan for achieving them, set a deadline,

---
Vision without action is a daydream. Action without vision is a nightmare.

Japanese proverb
---

visualize the results, and go after them. Doubtless you've heard the aphorism: *What gets written down gets done.*

Can you describe the life/lifestyle you seek?
You are going to have to tease out the building blocks of this kind of structured relationship. You can't *drift* into a Master/slave relationship. You will have to design this lifestyle – you can't just go along for the ride. That brings us to a question:

- In life, are you *proactive* or *reactive*? If you tend to be *reactive,* then what consequences might that have for your M/s relationship?

- Have you written down your goals for the next five or ten years? How does a slave or two fit into that vision? For example, if your vision is to live in a beautiful mountain cabin overlooking a lake and far away from a city, how does that mesh with your slave's thirst for big-city living, nice restaurants and theater?

- How's your imagination? Can you *think outside of the box?* To use Meyers-Briggs language, are you a "concrete-solid" thinker or a "creative risk-taker?" Do you have experience taking your vision and moving it to reality? (If the answer is "no," then you may want to consider books/courses that can train you in this art form. Hint: it has to do with *clarity of purpose* and *intent.* The key question is: "What are you willing to pay to get X result?" "Pay" means time and effort, as well as money. There's a *cost* to recreating yourself.)

By the way, if the words within the parentheses in that last paragraph whizzed by you, you may want to spend a bit more time on them. In my experience, the ability to create my own world is among my most valuable skills.

- Do you read much? Fiction? Non-fiction? What do you do with your knowledge? That is, do you keep knowledge to yourself or do you have a way of giving back to your community?

> When I examine myself and my methods of thought, I come to the conclusion that the gift of fantasy has meant more to me than my talent for absorbing positive knowledge.
> Albert Einstein

- Can you translate your ideas into words? How can you communicate your vision to your partner?

How clearly can you describe the PERSON you seek?

- What are you seeking in a slave? What kind of slave?

If the slave is not a vanilla (non-kinky) boyfriend or girlfriend, what IS your slave to be??? Pleasure slave (play partner)? Service slave (servant)? Business helper? Companion/lover?

- What is your slave seeking in a Master? What kind of Master? Companion for their future? A sage/teacher/mentor to rely upon? A path for sexual release? Financial and/or emotional security? A life-travel buddy? A spiritual guide? Leather? Why?

- Does *what you offer* match *what your slave seeks*? Financial or emotional stability? Sense of purpose? Adventure? Great sex? How are your assets? Can you afford to remake your slave (or slave-under-consideration) in your image?

- How smart, lucid, and articulate must your partner be? Does *quickness* matter to you? Does it matter that your partner can explain him/herself succinctly and with precision and clarity? Speaking personally, *quickness* matters a great deal to me. So does vocabulary level. IQ primarily helps people get quickly to answers – it's a "crunching power" issue. In that light, it may be reasonable for you to be concerned about IQ because the intellectual demands you can make on someone with an IQ of 100 will be different than you can make on someone with an IQ of 135.

- Do you want to have *shared values* with this person? Rather than a general "yes," let's explore...

I would propose that at some point in your M/s relationship you sit down with your partner – or partner-to-be – and probe how each of you feels about words that describe values. You might want to create a *values list* – very much like a pre-play negotiations checklist. Consider it a *pre-M/s relationship checklist*. And there are no right or wrong answers. For example, my own values concerning *biological family* and *orderliness* are substantially different from those of my slave. This is simply *information.* Discussing these points helped us to understand our reactions to the other on these specific points.

Here is the start of a list to consider. You will have to find longer lists from which to create your own list, this is just a starting point for thinking about *values.* An Internet search produces dozens of exhaustive lists from which to work.

Accuracy	Discipline	Harmony with others
Adventure	Efficiency	Honesty
Beauty	Excellence of work quality	Honor, honor code
Cleanliness, orderli-ness	Fairness	Independence
Community	Faith, spirituality	Inner peace, calm
Competence	Family	Justice, fair play
Concern for others	Feelings, emotions	Innovation
Cooperation – team spirit	Fun, happy, light-hearted	Integrity
Coordination	Global view of life	Knowledge
Decisiveness	Hard worker	Leadership

Once again, the goal, here, is to take each word on this (and your expanded) list and discuss it with your slave in order to learn more about your slave's (and your) basic beliefs. Since your basic beliefs color your everyday reality, the more you know about yourself and your slave, the better you'll be able to work together harmoniously.

What is a "Master" to you? What is a "slave"?

In my experience, relationships sometimes falter and fail because core values or basic assumptions differ between the partners. While each partner uses words such as "master" and "slave," they are unlikely to have a 100% match about what those words (and many other "concept words") actually mean. Unless the two of you sit down and carefully work through each other's personal values, traits, dreams, wants, and needs, there are likely to be recurring surprises as you get to know one another. The risk in NOT working through this exercise is that each of you may have been attracted to the superficial representation of the other person – you've been drawn to your partner's "public face," rather than to the person's "core being." While that may not be a bad thing, it may lead you to have to re-evaluate and re-adjust your on-going relationship more than you had initially expected.

While hardly an exhaustive list, here are some ideas about what a Master candidate might look like to a slave-in-waiting:

- Someone who understands that an M/s relationship is between equals – that the slave has no less value as a person than Master.

- A person who admits his/her personal weaknesses and is committed to turning those weaknesses into strengths and growing emotionally and spiritually.

- Someone emotionally, physically, and intellectually equal to or stronger than the slave.

- Someone to be responsible for the slave's wellbeing and the wellbeing of the relationship.

- A person who enough life experience, knowledge, and wisdom to serve as a mentor and teacher.

- A person who will hold the slave accountable to higher standards. This includes a Master who is spiritually awake and uses the M/s relationship to further spiritual development.

- A person who establishes an atmosphere of safety, even as he/she must discipline the slave for transgressions.

- A high-level communicator who maintains well-defined boundaries regarding accepted behavior.

- Someone who will be honest, even when knowing that the slave's reaction might be negative.

- A person who can demonstrate his/her understanding of the gift that is offered when total submission, obedience and service is given.

Here are some ideas about what a slave candidate might look like to a Master. Again, this is just a starting point. You have to make your own list.

- A person **experienced in the Leather culture**, who understands the demands of a structured relationship. Again, the fantasy of living 24/7 in a structured relationship is certainly going to differ from the fantasies described in books such as, The Sleeping Beauty trilogy (Anne Rice), or even the Marketplace series (Laura Antoniou).

- **A quick learner**. Someone who is likely to be adaptable to new situations. Someone who can apply knowledge to behavior. This describes a person in control of him/herself – not a person over-controlled by prior experiences. Let's face it; we all have baggage. Some people hang on to their baggage more than others. It's important when exploring an M/s relationship that the slave has the capacity to meld his/her world to the likes/dislikes of Master independent of the slave's own historical likes/dislikes. This takes flexibility.

- An **adventuresome** person who is committed to supporting you and your endeavors, regardless of where they lead.

- A person of **high moral/ethical behavior** who is also a clear communicator. This person must have the moral courage to be able to point out to Master behaviors of Master that concern the slave.

- Someone who has **experience serving others** and who demonstrates empathy and nurturing skills.

- Someone who **looks for the positives** in every situation. This person can be described variously as "A glass half-full person" or a "towards" person rather than an "away-from" person. Let me explain this one. In a general way, people tend either to reach towards new experiences or to react by turning away from new experiences. Some people embrace change, some resist change. Often, you will find that an attorney who is a litigator is a "towards" person, but a contracts attorney is an "away-from" person. Similarly, accountants are often "away-from" people. In business, "away-from" people are concerned about protecting their client's interests or their own business position. In business, "towards" people are often found to be the visionary leaders. When you put two "away-from" people together, they tend to avoid risk-taking and – consequently – may not have many adventures. When you put two "towards" people together, they may engage in very exciting, but also very risky, behavior. Which brings us to the next bullet:

- Someone with **well-defined boundaries**; someone who is clear about establishing boundaries. Combining this idea with the previous bullet, you can imagine two visionaries who are always out seeking new sensations and experiences, yet, who do this carefully and with appropriate discretion. Similarly, you can imagine two visionaries with poor boundary-setting skills that are so far out there that it makes others uncomfortable to be around them.

- A person with **wide-ranging skills in personal service**, plus, what I call, courtesan skills. These are skills of dressing well, music, dance, discourse, oral recitation and conversation. Among the personal service skills, I would include high-level executive secretary skills, the ability to manage a small business, the ability to represent Master in professional settings, and so forth.

Have you ever considered what you simply WON'T accept in a partner?

Topics in this arena are intended to be viewed in two ways: first, as part of the screening process a Master or slave would go through when considering a potential partner; and second, a nudge to look at your OWN behavior – whether or not you are in an established relationship.

You may find it useful to think through areas in which personal behavior would actually affect your willingness (or another's willingness) to start or to maintain an M/s relationship. I will skip the really obvious *character flaw* issues (dishonest, untrustworthy, etc.) and touch only on a few of the more subtle topics.

- **Personal habits:** A bit too messy? Compulsively clean? These are the little things that can wear on a partner. For example, if you open a kitchen cabinet and see things stuffed in there, do you care? What about the orderliness of your closet – or your slave's side of the closet? What about your underwear drawer or your slave's bedside table?

  Here's a practical example from my life with my own slave. When one walks into our bedroom, the power cords for electrical apparatus are visible under my slave's bedside table. Their appearance is an issue for me. In my home, all visible electrical cords are laced, rather than piled in an unsightly tangle. I required my slave to lace the cords. But, requiring this is a two-edged sword – which is why I use this example. On the one hand, I have standards of neatness that simply **will** be adhered to. On the other hand, my slave has to be willing to put up with my level of detail. In this case, I felt that my slave had enough "getting to know you" time during our first year together to figure out whether or not it would be possible to alter and adapt **her** lifetime of habits to **my** lifetime of habits. You, as Master, will have to make similar decisions concerning a wide array of **your slave's** behaviors. You have to pick your fights.

- **Personal presentation – grooming and dress**: One dresses (or, at least one should dress) in a manner intended to attract someone who would dress similarly. If you're looking for someone who likes to hang out at shopping malls, then blue jeans are your ticket. If you're looking for someone who likes to hang out at a four-star hotel lobby, blue jeans are **not** your ticket. I have a friend whose submissive will ONLY wear black and will ONLY wear spike heels. Hard limits. Deal breaker. One of the first things she negotiated with him. Sound silly or inconsequential? That depends upon your personal lifestyle. There are situations in life where wearing 5-inch spiked heels and dressing entirely in black makes you really, really stand out. Think "wedding," or "seaside resort," or "summertime in Glacier Park at the elegant lodge for dinner." Can you live with this or something similar? I know a Dom in our local BDSM community who insists that nobody can tell him how to dress. I've seen him show up in blue jeans at a rather formal dinner party. Everyone else was in full fetish costuming. You can draw your own conclusions.

- **Correct use of English**: In the same way that one dresses in a manner to attract a partner with similar tastes, the way you speak telegraphs your background – and that will be tied to a number of compatibility issues. I started life as a high school English teacher. When I hear someone using regional grammar ("I'd like **for** you to go to the market, please."), I notice it. If someone uses incorrect English ("Jim **ain't** got a chance of making that shot."), I notice it. If someone uses the wrong word ("Please keep me **appraised** of the situation."), I notice it. And I will say, personally, that imprecise English is on my list of "hard limits" for a partner.

- **Social manners/poise/personal mannerisms**: Do you notice if a person wipes his/her mouth with a linen table napkin or pats his/her mouth? Do you care if a person (of either gender) plops down in a chair or couch, rather than lowering him/herself into place? Do you notice whether women cross their ankles when seated or cross their legs? Do you notice whether a woman is wearing hose with her sandals? What images are YOU projecting that would attract a person with the type of social manners that you seek? And before you jump in and say that this doesn't apply to you, mentally transport yourself to some extreme subculture – Borneo tribe, or inner-city ghetto, or elite country club in Beverly Hills.

- **Sexual aptitude, appetite, and preferences**: Are you a match or mismatch? In the early flush of a relationship, one is inclined to overlook some issues. "I wish she dressed up a bit more," or "I wish he didn't slurp his coffee," or "I wish she wouldn't drive so fast." But, these can be handled through protocols within the context of an M/s relationship. Not so for sex. If one partner's idea of sex is five minutes of fucking and the

An M/s Studies Book

other person's is a two-hour sexual marathon, there's bound to be a problem – and it may not be very resolvable. If one partner is extremely sexually experienced and the other partner is not, there's bound to be a problem – again, it may not be very resolvable, even with communication and counseling.

The problem with resolving sexual compatibility issues is that we're not taught much about how to coach people in this arena. So, women fake orgasms and men resort to finding other ways of feeling fulfilled. For those of us who live in the world of BDSM play, issues of sexual compatibility become even more complicated. What if your slave needs to be spanked/caned/flogged to get warmed up before serious rough sex that involves face slapping, but **your** ideal evening consists of spending an hour or so tying up your slave in an elaborate shibari rope harness and then just sitting there watching him/her twist slowly from the suspension rig?

And what is "sex" for you, anyway? I have a friend for whom "sex" is fisting a woman without using lube. He loves to hear her scream. It turns him on, and it is an important part of their sexual dance; he claims that he prefers it to penile penetration. If I hadn't watched it, I wouldn't have believed it. My point, here, is that because we're kinky, we may have unusual sexual practices that require searching for that *special someone*, in order to get our needs fulfilled. And because of this, you have to decide whether your partner's "sexual preferences" fall into the "oh, I don't think so" category, or – being ever creative – you want to maintain the M/s relationship with this person, but bring in a *third* for some of the special sexual stuff.

What will you pay – in time and money – to make your relationship magical?
Okay, we've now explored questions about what you're looking for – in lifestyle and in the person – so, now it's time to ask how

36

Master/slave Relations

much are you willing to *pay* to get what you want? Don't for one minute think I'm speaking solely of what it's going to cost you to get your *partner* to operate in the fashion YOU wish – that's only half of it. It is very likely going to take time and money in order to add to your own personal skills and those of your mate. It takes a certain amount of anguish to move yourselves from being two individuals to being a *team.* One model to consider, here, would be *Marine Boot Camp.* Master may have to learn some serious personnel management techniques, but the slave not only has to master routine protocols (see either: <u>Protocols: Handbook for the female slave</u> or <u>Protocol Handbook for the Leather slave: Theory and Practice</u> by Robert J. Rubel, PhD), but also has to master immediate and graceful obedience to Master's commands. As we're not brought up in a culture where these behaviors are expected (think *Oriental),* this may take some patience over time.

Do you currently describe your life and your relationship(s) as *magical?* If not, you probably have not taken some quiet time to imagine a more romantic and exciting life. Chances are that you feel *at the effect* of having to work and live in a city in America, while being involved with your particular partner. What I mean by *at the effect* is that you are not at the *cause:* you have adjusted to the condition, rather than adjusting the condition to meet your needs.

This last point brings us back to the *imagination* issue raised in an earlier part of this book. You have to be able to conceive of something – you have to be able to write it out as a goal – in order to make it real. Many things first have to be thought out before they can be converted to reality. Said differently, if you don't hold the *concept* of something, it's hard to dream it up. There are many common examples of this when it comes to for-eign languages. Many languages have some words that don't exist in other languages. Just to make the point, you've prob-ably heard that some Eskimo languages have something like 60

37

terms describing various forms of snow and ice. In English, we sort-of have "slush, wet snow, snow, dry powder and ice." Those are about all we need in an industrialized nation. But, we'd be in trouble trying to understand an Eskimo's concern about the impending weather based on a discussion of the snow/ice conditions.

Similar blind spots creep into relationships. If you can't imagine a different set of conditions, then you can't work toward them. In my personal life, I have many times joined some group simply because it was *against my nature* to join such a group. I was in Rotary International for many years for that reason. I joined a square dance club – and lasted five years – for that reason. I will sometimes explore a new relationship with someone who does NOT fit my personal sense of a "good fit" for that reason.

So, my message is: work to stretch your experiences so that you

> The danger lies in imprisoning ourselves within our definitions of experience.
>
> David Boorstein, Librarian of Congress

can grow your imagination; the richer your imagination, the richer your life.

I used the *training contract* time with my slave to consider one single question: does this person have the raw potential to become my *model slave?* My rather coarse expression for this is: *You can't make a silk purse out of a sow's ear, unless you start with a silk sow.*

For me, the issues were these:

- Is the slave smart enough?
- Is the slave *willing?* (Hello, Master Steve Sampson)
- Will the slave obey?
- Is the kind of service the slave offers the kind of ser-

vice that I want?

- Will the slave accept a polyamorous/swinging lifestyle on top of the M/s dynamic?

Once I had my answer, I made my own commitments:

- My slave moved in with me as soon as that was feasible;

- I supported a decision that my slave not work in order that she spend workdays gaining skills I wanted from my slave. (If you've read my Protocols book, you realize that my slave's role in my life is that of my Personal Assistant. Her duties include serving as my *Major Domo, valet, butler, chef, chauffeur, secretary, nurse,* and *research assistant,* as well as my *courtesan.*)

So, one of the threshold questions is this: Is your interest in an M/s structure a permanent lifestyle issue, or are you exploring M/s structures as a form of scene-specific BDSM play? What's your level of commitment?

Let me address this topic to two distinct audiences: those readers who are currently in an M/s relationship, and those who are reading this book and considering whether or not to enter into an M/s relationship.

If you are **currently** in an M/s relationship, the *investment* question probably centers on your mutual growth or on skills that your slave could attain that would benefit your relationship or please you as Master. This endless list could include topics such as:

- Learn something about investing. (real estate, stock market, etc.)

- Run a small business.

- Entertain more formally.

- Play sports of some kind.
- Learn massage therapy.
- Participate in international travel.
- Learn to dance.
- Attend self-improvement courses or focused business-skills courses (speaking, running a meeting, time management, personnel management).
- Improve cooking skills.
- Get certified in advanced first aid and CPR.
- Become a master at giving sexual pleasure – strengthen your pelvic floor muscles (either gender, actually), fellatio skills, etc.
- Prepare a "slave's Book" that records all Master's particular preferences – create checklists for all repeatable processes (packing before a trip, preparing for a dinner party, etc.).

Now, let me approach an answer for this section of the book for those of you who are **exploring** the idea of starting an M/s relationship. I'll assume that you've obtained this book because you think that a *structured relationship* makes sense for you. If you're at the front-end of a relationship, you have some time to consider some *big picture* issues. My strong recommendation is to write out – as clearly as possible – what you absolutely **must** have in a slave (or a Master). Write out those skills you want this person to possess – then look for a person with most or all of those skills already in hand. This is a far more rapid and less costly process than taking a person and retraining them in your image. Importantly, because of the *authority exchange* aspect of an M/s relationship, the slave is not in a very good position to retrain Master.

So, let's consider that you are *exploring* an M/s relationship. You're toying with the idea. But, you've run into a problem.

You've been *looking for a slave (or a Master)* for some time – perhaps years – and for some reason, you've not been able to make it work.
Hmmmmm.

This could be time for a little introspection. Perhaps you need to consider seriously examining yourself. You need to do this *for yourself* and not for some possible future partner. You'll have to make a list that is personally relevant, but for starters…

- How's your English – both oral and written? Would you be at home in a graduate-school discussion of some topic, or would you draw attention to yourself?

- How are your table manners? Know how to pick up a fork? Know how to pat (not *wipe*) *your* mouth with a napkin? Know not to open that napkin more than half way? Know where to place the napkin when you arise from Table?

- When you enter a room, do you take a moment to check it out? Do you immediately recognize whether or not the room's owner is *highly visual*? Are you able to make distinctions about the owner's social class and personal tastes from the room decorations? Why do this? So you can establish rapport during conversations.

- When you speak, is your voice gentle and pleasing? Do you have a nasal tonality? Have a regional dialect?

- If you hear something spoken, can you identify/isolate key issues and repeat them with accuracy?

- How's your wardrobe? Do you dress fashionable or are you fashion challenged.

- How *flexible* are you, psychologically – can you adapt quickly to changing circumstances, or do you *freeze in the headlights?* (I don't mean *crises,* I mean long-wave life changes. Job retraining, for example.)

- How are you at *conversational magic?* Do you know enough about social intercourse not to speak only about *yourself?* Can you enthrall a slave candidate (or a Master candidate) for hours by asking leading questions? How broadly can you speak about current events?

- When you are out in public, how closely do you notice people? Do you notice their gestures, their expressions, their mannerisms? To monitor the slave, the Master must be an extremely keen observer.

- How much Leather history do you know? After all, this is a *Leather lifestyle.*

- How good are you at problem solving? Ever read any books about it? Same for *branch thinking* vs. *linear thinking.* Can you "think outside of the box" when solving problems?

- Do you watch TV? Consider limiting your viewing time and reading more books. Read widely and learn to discuss what you read. Consider joining a book club. Learn to prepare two and three course meals for yourself. It's a skill you may need later. Never dine informally when alone. Bad habit. No, I have not changed viewpoints; I'm still addressing Masters. This is all about building up the little personal habits – the "muscle memory" – to Master someone else.

- Are you an expert in some form of BDSM play? Okay, so master another form of BDSM play. And who, if I may be so bold, agrees with you that you ARE a Master at some form of BDSM? Does your local kink group ask you to do presentations?

- Do you have a spiritual core? How does your spirituality influence/affect/alter your life?

- Do you have good anger management? Are you carrying difficult *baggage* from your childhood or prior marriage? Have you considered seeing a therapist? Too expensive? Just how costly is it for you NOT to deal with your baggage?

- Learn to interrupt what you are doing, start something else, then come back to what you were doing. When you own a slave, you will need to be sensitive to managing that person's time. You should learn how it feels to be interrupted in the middle of a task that you are completing from a list of perhaps a dozen other tasks that all must be completed.

- Learn to do things *completely* and *perfectly*. After all, you are likely to demand that level of activity from your slave – so, be able to lead by example. If you are doing dinner dishes, end by scouring the counters and sinks. If you are making notes on how to *do something,* make the notes neat and put them in your protocol book. In this way, when you find your slave candidate, you can

---

The greatest incentive for a Master to expand skills and experiences is that the new you will likely attract a more versatile slave.

Bob Rubel

---

show this person your protocol book, based upon your own mastery of a skill set.

I'll stop. I could go on, and so could you. This is really a small part of what you are going to have to put yourself through to reinvent yourself in the image you think your partner-to-be would be seeking.

What if it Doesn't Work?
I've put this section in this part of the book because it's part of *knowing one's self.*

> You have to know when to hold 'em, know when to fold 'em, know when to walk away, know when to run...
>
> Kenny Rogers, The Gambler

To quote Master Skip Chasey: "A Master is willing to bear, without complaint or self-pity, the awareness that doing his best may at times not be good enough." (Master Skip Chasey: *The Qualities of a Master*)

And, let me hasten to add: when a relationship doesn't work out in an M/s structure, one option is to change the structure! After all, you must have felt something *substantial* to have offered (or accepted) the training contract in the first place. Build on the common elements, rather than dismiss the entire relationship. Don't throw the baby out with the bathwater.

Personally, I have had the experience of extending a three-month training contract to a potential slave, only to discover, at about the 60-day point, that the person did not have a slave heart. She wanted the relationship to work so badly that she worked very hard to conform to my version of an M/s relationship; we realized we were on the wrong path. However, rather than end our relationship, we restructured it as a form of Daddy/girl relationship (ours was an Uncle/niece structure). This worked just fine and lasted another nine months. This structure had the added advantage of being much less threatening to my Alpha slave.

But, if the relationship *does* have to end, if you can't agree on a different structure, all your friends need to know is that *the contract ended*. Nothing else. "Didn't you want to renew it?", asked a well-meaning friend. "No, we were **complete** with our relationship, and the contract period ended." End of story.

Chapter Summary

In Part I, we started out by defining the common terms for players in this M/s sphere – Master, Dom, submissive and slave, to name a few. Then we rolled through some common relationship structures – Top/bottom, Dom/submissive, Master/slave, and Owner/slave. In Part II, we proposed some self-examination questions. We asked you to consider who YOU are and what you SEEK. We asked how much you would PAY – in time and money – to transform yourself and/or your slave to be your ideal person, and ended that part of the book by suggesting ways of changing a relationship that didn't quite work out.

An M/s Studies Book

"Master/slave relationships are about understanding who we are on earth and what we are here to do."

Master Jim Glass,
Northeast Master/slave Conference, 2006

Part III: Grappling with Elements of the

Relationship

Okay, you've decided to prepare for an M/s relationship. Before we get into selecting a partner, there are a few preparatory thoughts.

Why Does This Person Want to be a slave?

You might want to explore a threshold question: does your slave candidate want to be a 24/7 slave or something else? For the sake of this section, I'll assume you want what is increasingly called, *Total Power Exchange* – a 24/7 relationship that involves power exchange, as opposed to scene-specific role-play. From this point, the greatest hurdle is the candidate's personal honesty. You are going to have to discern what sings to this person – what he/she really wants out of this relationship with you. Is

---

The slave's role is to be of service to Master.

That's it.

That's the slave's reason for being.

The trick, then, is to be a Master worthy of such service.

The trick is to be a Master who offers so much – in terms of life experiences and personal support – that the slave's service is more than justified.

Bob Rubel

---

this slave really prepared for an *authority exchange* in which you, as Master, now have nearly absolute control? You may want your slave candidate to think this through for a minute. The slave may love jazz, and Master only listens to rap. How will that work? In fact, how will your candidate react when you elect not to allow your slave to listen to the radio or to CDs at all? Be assured, I decide on my slave's wardrobe, hair color and style, nail color, car choice, and use of time.

And, this is NOT *micromanagement.* It's a case of the Master wishing his/her life to *be* a certain way and using the slave to support those intentions. Is your candidate clear that once he/she enters into a Master/slave relationship 24/7, all rights to make personal choices are forfeit? For example, if your slave

---

Critical Observation: As a general rule, "A" leaders select "A" players because they are confident in their own abilities and are used to being surrounded by excellence. However – again as a general rule – "B" leaders select "C" players because they can't risk being exposed as "B" leaders rather than as "A" leaders.

---

tells you that he/she is going out on errands to point A, B and C, I expect that YOU expect that the slave will only to go to points A, B and C. How are you going to react if your slave decides to stop in at point D? Do you take that as a good sign of initiative, or do you take it as an incredible exercise of free will? Do you expect a phone call from the slave asking whether or not you will allow him/her to add in the extra stop, or are you satisfied so long as the slave explains why the extra stop was necessary? (My answer, by the way, was that the extra stop was an incredible and inexcusable exercise in the very kind of free will that the slave no longer possesses. The slave made that stop by taking time away from me.)

Of course, this is what we're discussing throughout this book.

On Ego and Insecurity in Relationships

Okay, I'm going to go out on a limb, here. I'm going to apply some really sensitive business wisdom to choosing a mate in an

M/s setting. I'm not sure whether I hope nobody reads this, or whether I hope a lot of people read this. But, I will say this: when I began looking for a slave, I specifically looked for an "A" type.

In a business environment, this plays out as follows: It's better to have an "A" team with a "B" plan, than a "B" team with an "A" plan. This business idea probably was derived from an old Arab proverb: *An army of sheep lead by a lion would defeat an army of lions led by a sheep.* In a personal environment, my experience is that an insecure Dom will take a **weaker, less secure submissive** as a partner in order to be able to control the person without being "called" on his act. (Note: I'm using *Dom/submissive,* rather than *Master/slave,* because I've never seen this phenomenon in an M/s relationship.)

I've actually seen this situation unfold in real life. A close friend of mine was faced with having to choose to marry one of two women. Although successful in business and investments, he selected the weaker, less self-actualized woman because he, himself, was insecure about relations with women. His choice astonished his close friends at the time. The woman could never quite get on the same page with him; he finally gave up trying and resigned himself to the situation. (Recall my earlier story about silk purses and sows ears.)

On *Emotions* in Relationships

Clearly a truism, there are substantial differences between men and women raised in Western civilization when it comes to accessing and expressing emotions. Thus, it will also be a truism that the *emotional structure* of an M/s relationship in the Western world will *feel* quite different, depending upon the gender structure:

- Male Master, male slave
- Male Master, female slave
- Female Master, female slave

- Female Master, male slave
- Yes, I know it's not this simple – but you get the idea

People vary in the degree to which they can access and rely upon their own emotions. Some people tend mostly to *think* about their relationships with others; other people tend more easily to *feel* their relationships with others. When stress enters the M/s relationship, these differences can become exaggerated. There are many great books out there that explore this area, and I would encourage you to do this. Some suggested readings are:

- Gray, John. <u>Men Are from Mars, Women Are from Venus: The Classic Guide to Understanding the Opposite Sex</u>. New York, NY: HarperCollins, 1992.
- Chapman, Gary D. <u>The Five Love Languages: How to Express Heartfelt Commitment to Your Mate</u>. Northfield Publishing; Reissue edition, 1995.

Side note: I suspect that there are gender-linked differences that concern one's access to one's emotions, and also to the emotional reactions, themselves. This particularly comes into play when Master starts talking about multiple slaves or polyamory. Translation: I think that a discussion about multiple sex partners is going to be received differently by slaves of different genders. But, I could be wrong.

On the Role of *Love* in the M/s Relationship

There is quite an active controversy within the M/s movement about the role of love. On the one hand, some Masters take the position that love contaminates the M/s dynamic because Master can never be sure whether or not the slave is complying with a request/Instruction out of <u>love</u>, or out of <u>obedience</u>. Since obedience is the core of the M/s dynamic, Master would lose the capacity to monitor the slave's core reactions.

On the other hand, many Masters feel that if they're going to put all the time and effort into training a slave with whom they will spend lots of time, they want to be submerged in a loving relationship with that person. But, a loving relationship is not necessarily a girlfriend/boyfriend relationship, and the Master may want to carefully consider whether to suppress the tendency for slaves to think of their Master as their "girlfriend" or "boy-friend." "Girlfriend/boyfriend" relationships belong to the Vanilla World – the not-kinky world – along with relationships with other family members, especially children. These relationships should be kept separate, as they do not involve the authority or power exchanges inherent in D/s and M/s relationships.

Disclaimer #1: When you label someone this way, your decision must be based upon your own personal observations, not on hearsay. Beware of repeating gossip. Also, you need to consider what you will do if you're accused of traits such as these.

Disclaimer #2: No, I'm not thinking of any real person; but if you think I'm describing you, you may – in fact – have a problem.

Also, there can be substantial differences between "the Master's love" and "the slave's love." The Master is more likely to love the slave – rather than be "in love" with the slave. However, the slave will probably fall "in love" with Master. This situation, where the Master "loves" the slave and the slave is "in love" with the Master, can lead to some potential misunderstandings and stress unless discussed openly and with truthfulness. It may be useful to discuss different forms of love with a prospective slave, lest they confuse your relationship.

Are You Sure You're a Good Master?

Most people are pretty sure that they're Okay. Most people think that most others are also pretty much Okay. But, some people think that certain people are **not** Okay. The thing of it is, the person who *you think is not so Okay* probably thinks he's just fine. So, let me explore this a little.

Our Community – and here I'm combining the Leather and the Not-Leather BDSM Communities – contains mostly bright, dynamic and interesting people. It also contains some really average people. And, too, it contains some icky people. As I just mentioned, **they** probably won't think of themselves as presenting problems within the Community, but others do. To describe these folks, Jay Wiseman coined the phrase: *Poor Quality Dominants* (PQDs). I have also heard this topic discussed at Leather Leadership conferences. Consider whether you know someone with these characteristics:

- This person is quick to categorize other Doms in his Community as, *Poor Quality Dominants,* and he works to isolate them. (That is, the very fact that he categorize people this way should be a red flag about *his own* attitudes and actions. Sure, there may actually be a few people in the Community who genuinely cause trouble – but, they are rare and will be broadly recognized for what they are within the Community.)

- He tends to try to dominate other Doms. He finds that he has a little clique of *warriors* around him who are quick to exclude others from his group. He tends to feel that his way is the right way and other ways are *less than* his correct way.

- He declines to take counsel from Seniors – those who have been in the scene a long time – because he consider himself to be a Senior, and thus, dosen't have to listen to anyone.

- He engages in self-aggrandizement. He takes credit

where credit is **not** due. He claims to have started an organization, but he didn't. He starts calling himself Master XYZ – but no Senior Leather Master will respect that self-appointed title. He bought his own Master's cap.

- He has a tendency to *take his ball and walk off the court* if he can't control a group or a situation. Closely allied: people around him feel that they must do things your way *or it's the highway.* He mostly cooperates in situations that benefits him.

- He has a very small and tight-knit circle of friends who seem not to last very long. He constantly throws friends out of his *inner circle* for various reasons; He has a string of *previous friends* trailing behind him. If he wanted to give a party, his first thought would not be "Gosh, where can I find a place big enough?", or would it be "Gosh, who would I want to spend the evening with?", or – worse yet – "Who would want to spend the evening with me?"

- He is so jealous, so protective of his slave/submissive, that he restrict his or her appearance at kink-related events unless he is also present. Related to this, he his so afraid of what an ex-lover (or ex-slave) will say about him within his Community, that he trashes this person's reputation before they have a chance even to realize he dumped them.

- He spends his energies spreading gossip that is negative about the good works of others within the Community, rather than creating his own works, projects, or organizations. If he does build his own organization, it's a sham: its real purpose is to have a vehicle that he can brag about of as his own, rather than as a positive force in the Community. He may be known for trying to take over another organization after being (at last) cast out of the previous one.

- He's found himself repeatedly embroiled in some local controversy or flare-up – often on an e-group.

- His admirers are all *very junior* in the Community. Those who know him are somewhat *polite, but distant.*

The message, here, is that while some people may exhibit one or two of the characteristics in this list (yes, I'm being charitable), if you know someone with many of these characteristics, then this person may not be very *in touch* with what others within the Community think of him. He may have something of a *tainted* reputation and not really know it. Interestingly, it's been my repeated experience that people who exhibit a number of these characteristics have such thorough psychological barriers to meaningful self-examination, that they have elaborate ways to explain and justify the controversies they foment. They see their lack of friends and their difficulty in finding or keeping a slave as being a problem/flaw in **others**. Attempts to aid and counsel people with these kinds of blinders will only get you cast out along with the others from their past. Typically, these are very, very angry people.

So, did you recoil at this list? That's OK. I put it here so you could be aware of these and simular traits when it comes to selecting a slave or a Master. You need to find out your candidate's *track record.* You need to do some research into the congruency between what the person **says**, and what the person **does**. I'll touch on this a bit later.

On Choosing a Mate

I'm going to begin this part of the book by taking a broader view of the M/s relationship and concentrate on some lessons from the "Vanilla" world – slightly augmented by my own comments. On several occasions, I've watched negotiations for an M/s relationship break down when the Master would present the potential slave with a long list of *demands and conditions* prior to spending any time with the person to determine whether or not they even wanted a relationship with them to begin with. Said differently, the Master wanted the slave candidate to skip the "getting to know you" stage of relationship-building in favor of the "here's how you must obey me, *or else*" stage. Needless to say, these "Masters" spent a lot of time churning through slave candidates.

So, here, for your consideration, are some general relationship guidelines that apply both to the Master and to the slave:

1. **Attributes:** Think of yourself as an older Master. Think of yourself as 75. Okay, try 83. You're probably not having much sex. Your slave's skin is getting thin and fragile, so you have had to stop the flogging; whips went away years ago. What's remaining? What *core values* do you want to rely upon? You have to make this list. I can only posit the situation.

   Flip the situation. You're still the 75 year-old Master being viewed through your slave's eyes: what core values and steady behaviors bind the two of you? When your slave reflects on the last five years, does he/she express a dreamy and satisfied look of fulfillment, or a hardened look of a life not lived very satisfyingly.

   So, here is a little list of personal attributes for you to consider:

   - Kindness
   - Loyalty
   - Insight
   - Flexibility/adaptability
   - Devotion
   - Ability of the mate to take care of him/herself

2. **Inquisitiveness:** When you expect to be with someone a

long time, you may want someone who goes out into the world and brings back ideas for new experiences. You may get tired of doing all the leading. What characteristics would you want in a slave that supports that result?

- Can the person expand to develop their potentials?
- Are they quick to want to learn new things?
- Can they see old things in new ways?
- Are they curious?

3. **Mutual attraction:** What brings the two of you together?

- Are YOU sensitive? Is this person *sensitive?* Is he/she alert to things around the two of you when you are together? **Are you interested in *how* your slave thinks, as much as *what* he/she thinks?** [This is a fine point, and I'll expand it a bit. In this country, the difference between the handful of elite private colleges and the vast number of *other* post-secondary institutions is that the elite institutions teach you *how to think,* while the others only offer courses about *what to think.* In my own relationship with my own slave, I am extremely concerned with *how* she thinks.]

- How do each of you react to the other person's personal space – home or apartment? Do each of you compliment the other on decorations, or are you (or your slave candidate) fairly oblivious to them? Because your personal décor is likely to be an expression of YOU, this is an important point.

4. **Processing emotional hurt:** When you hurt someone, they feel pain and show it. When they hurt you, they feel your pain. The question is: how do each of you care for the other when you've hurt one another? Effectively handling pain you cause another is an important aspect of maturity and vital in a stable relationship.

- Do you clam up – indicating that you don't know how to process the pain you have given your partner?

- Do you go into some form of stylized speech pattern, indicating immaturity?

Our Family uses the Native American process of "talking sticks" to work through upsets. Either the Master or slave may request a session. The hurt party picks up the stick and talks until he/she is done. The stick then passes to the other party, who speaks until done. The person holding the stick may not be interrupted. This goes on until the issue is resolved. Another Master who uses this system explained that over the years, in his Family, it got so that the talking sticks only had to be used when *both Master and slave* were emotionally involved with an issue. Otherwise, the person who was not the aggrieved party could easily sit quietly while the upset partner expressed his/her hurt.

5. **Independence:** Choose someone who has an inner life, someone on their own journey, someone independent of you. This person should see you as a partner on his or her journey.

   Personally, I distinguish between *wanting* and *needing* someone. If you *need them*, you are at the *effect* of the relationship – that is, you don't come from *choice* and you are unusually vulnerable. If you feel you *need* your mate, chances are you're going to run into some problems within an M/s structure.

6. **Passion:** Be passionate about something. And choose someone who has similar passions – similar interests in making memories. You may need to draw on the good memories during hard times. Choose someone who makes your life bigger, not smaller. Select a person who is curious about the world around them.

7. **Values:** Choose someone with similar values. There are many "relationship models," some of which are quite unusual. You should understand something about these

different models as early in the relationship as possible, and make sure your intended slave has both a similar understanding and a similar model in mind. At an extremely broad cut, some relationship models are:

- Open vs. closed sexual relationship (one or both partners can have other casual sexual partners)
- Mongamy vs. polyamory (multible long term partners)
- Power exchange vs. equal partners

8. **Compassion:** When you pass a poor person on the street (perhaps a "street person"), what is your reaction? What is your potential slave's reaction? Are you repulsed or do you feel empathy? In an important way, this reaction can be a proxy measure for a person's *openness*. (A *proxy measure* is an unrelated – but acceptable – question you can ask that actually answers another question.) You may find that a person who has trouble expressing compassion for others less fortunate may have trouble "plugging in" to YOU. Or, this may be an indicator that you may have trouble plugging in to your slave. Is your potential mate willing to listen to you? Truly listen? Do YOU listen? How do you know you're really listening?

9. **Processing/sorting modalities:** The best place to find out more information about this topic is to do an Internet search on NLP (Neuro-Linguistic Programming). This is a field unto itself and a course of study that I highly recommend for a Master. This will bring you very rewarding personal skills for working with people, whether or not this includes your slave. Basically, a person tends to process information cognitively, visually, auditorily, tactilely, or in some combination. For best effect, you will want to present information to people according to their preferred processing style. You can get an idea of their style by listening to their language (I *hear* what you say; I *see* what you mean; I *know* what you mean; I *feel* your pain; I *sense* that...)

As it applies in this book – and this list – you need to be sure you each understand the other's "sorting" styles. Equally, if not more importantly: Do you say "I love you" in a way that your partner can "get it?" (Although I've already mentioned it, see: Chapman, Gary D. <u>The Five Love Languages: How to Express Heartfelt Commitment to Your Mate.</u> Northfield Publishing; Reissue edition, 1995.)

- **Money/gifts:** Some men feel that turning their pay-checks over to their spouse, or buying gifts, is a demonstration of "I love you" and that they don't have to *say* anything.

- **Sensory:** Some people respond to verbal cues, some to touch, some to visual cues. Work this out before you take someone as your slave, or at least be able to "translate" for them.

- **Performing services:** Some people translate the neatness/tidiness of the house as *I love you*.

- **Time and attention:** Some people consider that spending a lot of time with them translates to, *I love you*.

- **Verbal:** Some people respond most strongly to being <u>told</u> that they are loved.

10. **Selective blindness:** Learn to overlook certain faults. Sometimes, little things that initially were attractive/cute will become annoying over time. I'm not suggesting that you overlook character flaws such as criminal activity or dishonesty; you can't build a relationship with someone once serious character flaws are revealed. But, I *am* suggesting that in the larger scope of your lives together, there may be certain annoyances that may be better left alone.

11. **Amicability:** Be able to laugh at yourself; have lots of friends. This usually indicates friendliness, flexibility and openness. Good attributes in a mate. You will appreciate these traits in a slave and your slave will appreciate these traits in you.

Some *New-Relationship* Distinctions

What ROLE do you want to play in this relationship?

- Boyfriend/girlfriend?
- Master/Mistress; Dom/Domme; Daddy or Top?
- submissive/boy/boi/girl or slave?

Related to this – are you interested in the ROLE, or in the PERSON, or both? What if the role doesn't work out? Remember the story I related a few pages back... I had started an M/s relationship with a woman that didn't work out, so we transformed it into an Uncle/niece role-play, and it worked just fine. So, are you flexible?

And, dare I ask: what if you are a *switch*?? What if you are BOTH switches? Now what role? Are you going to be Master some of the time and role-play submissive to your own slave? Are you firm enough in your Mastery to be willing to wear your slave's collar?

Have you ever considered playing more than one role at a time?

In large Households, Master can have a slave with whom he has sex, a slave only for service, and a puppy for a pet. Then, again, you may keep a boy/boi around who needs nurturing growth. As you earn respect within the Leather Tribe (the term many Leather folk use to describe their subculture), you might find that you are approached to Master one or more people who are seen less frequently than the household slaves. There are so many roles that one can play within the overall M/s dynamic, that I can't really do that topic justice. This is a world where you can stretch yourself. You can be different people to different people. You can express yourself differently as a function of your different relationships.

Within the M/s structure, what ACTIVITIES are you likely to pursue?
I know, you want it *all.* And, that is fine; it's just that you probably want more of one thing than another. The clearer you can be about what you want, the more likely you are to be able to find that mix in a person.

- **Vanilla** – So, you might want a *companion* to attend business functions and family events with you. Does that mean that you want a slave for whom SM play is a minor part of the sought-after relationship? Does this point to a relationship almost devoid of formal proto-cols?

- **Sex** – So, you might want someone really good at it that enjoys it the way you offer it. Does that mean that you are seeking a slave who has had vast prior sexual experiences, or does that mean that you want some-one without much sexual experience that you can train from the ground up?

- **Service** – So, someone with demonstrable service background is important. You may find that it's hard to take a doctor or lawyer and expect them to fit the role of chef and serving wench. On the other hand…

- **BDSM Play** – So, a masochist would be useful – a pain slut?

What AUTHORITY SYSTEM is involved?
This is a Master Jack McGeorge question, and I love it.

- **What are the *grounds* for your authority?** Did you declare it, or earn it? What, in your past, demonstrates that you can exert authority over another? Been a military officer? Been in business management? Made a lot of money? Been an Eagle Scout? You may find it easier to move into a Master's position if you exude demonstrable authority. Failing that, you may have to spend more time reinventing yourself – learning the myriad skills described in this book that will result in your ability to present yourself with authority and confidence.

- **How *broad* is your authority?** Do you intend to control your slave's finances? If so, are you willing to support your slave financially? Do you control your slave's access to his/her biological family? Again, this touches on the question of how much you are willing to spend to achieve the slave model you seek.

- **Do you distinguish between *punishment* and *correction?*** For example, my slave will only be *punished* for a violation of our contract – something extremely unlikely. On the other hand, I am not above *correcting* my slave for a variety of protocol violations.

  I write this with an important additional note: As slaves generally work very hard to please their Masters, I recommend administering correction very sparingly, lest your slave become overcritical of her/his own actions and wary of your scrutiny. **I also recommend that you be particularly careful to distinguish between correcting your slave's behavior, versus correcting your slave as a person.** You want to love and cherish the person, while correcting behavior.

How do you deal with Reactance and Resistance?
Sooner or later, you are going to encounter *reactance* and *resistance* from your slave. This is particularly true if you are living together. You give an order; your slave reacts to the order. This reaction can take the form of a look of defiance, a little expres-

sion of exasperation or disgust, a rolling of eyes, or a direct challenge that questions the order. This tends to be something that many D/s and M/s couples go through, particularly those who are living in a 24/7 M/s setting.

Perhaps the most common low-level problem occurs when the slave reacts with some vanilla-sounding reply such as: "Oh, sure. I'll go get it." When this happens in my personal relationship with my slave, I generally react by saying something like: "And how would that reply be phrased if you were in protocol?" That's generally enough to get my slave to recognize the lapse and to restate the sentence as: "Sir, yes Sir! I'll go get it, Sir."

But, stepping up the scale, the time will come when you issue an order and the slave reacts to it in a way that you feel must be addressed; that your failure to address the issue will degrade the nature of the authority-exchange upon which the relationship is based. In such a case, I recommend you consider what is called a *state change*. Here, you stop whatever is going on at the time and change both your physical position and your slave's physical position. Typically, I put my slave in Full Present position (on both knees hands locked behind back) and allow the slave time to reflect and to become more composed. This is a time for the slave to *refocus* and discuss the underlying cause of the reactance. A Master with an open mind and open heart will learn a great deal at this point – often about himself/herself, rather than about the slave.

Reactance, unaddressed, is likely, at some point, to become *resistance*. **Resistance** occurs when the submissive/slave resists Master's dominance – sometimes unconsciously. Now, you've got a problem. This is likely to be a substantial signal that something fundamental is amiss. This requires some careful probing and questioning. In my experience, when a slave gets to the point of demonstrating resistance, Master is being inattentive – Master is not hearing/seeing/feeling the slave's signals for help/relief on some front. Again, my continual theme: you need outstanding listening skills and an appreciation of the world through the slave's eyes.

How do you execute the responsibility of your command?
How do you demonstrate your Mastery (walk the talk) with integrity and honor?

This is another Master Jack McGeorge question and it's a window into another dimension – the dimension of personal mastery. Being a list kind of guy, I'm going to give my flavor of answer with a number of short topics that are augmented with bulleted notes. By the way, this presumes that you are living an exemplary values-centered life of honesty and integrity. This list is more about executing *your management responsibilities in an M/s relationship.*

Thinking of Yourself as a Business Leader
As Master, you're a manager. You're managing a piece of very pricey property – a *person.* That calls for use of some rather traditional management techniques. One technique involves *keeping your eye on the ball*, as it were.

A good manager asks the following questions every three months:

- What are my objectives for the next 90 days?
- What are my plans, priorities and hopes?
- How do I go about achieving them?

To avoid *drifting through life,* you might consider developing short review sessions every quarter and checking in with your slave. (Personally, I used to have annual planning meetings with my first wife. My father always found this astonishing.) Are you both on the same page? Are you doing what you need to do to reach your stated goals?

Here is a list of the more prominent traits of successful leaders. Successful leaders...

- Observe with application (they act on their observations).
- Take copious notes.
- Know how to listen well; know how to distinguish between background "chatter" and important issues; know how to ask clear, courteous and incisive questions.
- Welcome ideas.
- Value time highly.
- Set goals as a matter of routine.
- Try to understand a situation before commenting on it; they don't jump to conclusions.
- Always anticipate achievement.
- Know how to organize their approach to challenges; [This list to this point is attributed variously to Whitt N. Schultz and to H. Gordon Selfridge, and I've added some commentary].
- Have a five-year plan for success.
- Realize that they, not others, ultimately control their own success.
- Brainstorm alternatives to tough decisions (use *consensus management techniques – for more information Google "consensus management"*).
- Celebrate their achievements; shrug off their setbacks.
- Develop and use a support network.
- Always stand for integrity.
- Remind themselves that every day is a new opportunity.
- Keep themselves in top physical condition.
- Always remain open to learning new ideas [The lower part of the list is adapted from Bob Adams, *Streetwise Business Tips*. Adams Media Corp.].

Applying this last section to your M/s lifestyle, you might consider taking each of these bullet points and opening it up. Tease out the implications of each bullet for your personal situation. For example, take the bullet that reads: "Always anticipate achievement." What can this mean in your world? How well do you support your slave, emotionally? Are you always *catching him/her doing something right?* Do you bring home occasional treats/ gifts of love? Do you know your slave's favorite things – and do you make sure his/her favorites make it into your life, too? I know, sounds like a marriage. It's far more than that, of course – spousal support is only the support base for a highly evolved *structured relationship.*

The fact that you own a slave does not excuse you from reinforc- ing in your slave extreme feelings of love and warmth toward you as Master and an appreciation for how lucky your slave is that you accepted him/her. Often, my slave will ask me what I want for the evening. My unswerving answer is: "What I want is that tomorrow morning you open your eyes in bed and you say to me: 'Wow! What a fabulous night we had last night, thank you so much."

Chapter Summary

Okay, we've been grappling with some of the core elements of a relationship. I asked you to consider *why* this person wants to be a slave – in general – and YOUR slave, in particular. I spent some time discussing how ego and insecurity, love and emotions enter into relationships. Next, I challenged you to examine some possible negative features of your own personality and behavior, then moved on to describe some attributes you might want to consider when choosing a mate. From there, I asked you what *role* you intended to play within your M/s dynamic, what *activities* you were considering, and by what *authority system* you felt you were a Master. This part of the book ended with a discussion of ways you could possibly solidify or re-create yourself as a business leader – a business leader who owns a very valuable asset: a slave.

It is a widely-held dream among Leatherfolk and one that manifests itself in many ways both in fantasy and in reality. It is our subculture's expression of love and support, a beautiful variant on the ideal biological family combined with flavors of hippy communal living, an Arabian Nights harem, a pirate ship, and grandma's house all rolled into one.

Jack Rinella,
Leatherviews Issue number 40 (September 21, 2006)

Part IV: The Framework of the Relationship – Your Leather House

The *Leather Household* is one of the distinguishing characteristics of the Leather Lifestyle. It also distinguishes a Leather Master/ slave relationship from a Not-Leather M/s relationship. That is – the Leather Family lives and acts in the context of the customs and traditions of their own Leather Household. That Household (or *House*) is known by its characteristics. These characteristics fall into certain general categories:

- Household creed and protocols
- Expectations governing family behavior
- Expectations about responsibilities and duties inside and outside the House
- Beliefs – not only about the spiritual side of life, but also about people
- Agreements and time commitments

Household Credo and Related Protocols

I'll start this section by pointing out that when it comes to establishing your Leather Household, you – as Master – are going to have to grapple with how you intend to translate your own vision of **yourself** into actions and protocols that express *who you are* to the outside world. That is, you are going to need to translate your core values to visible actions through protocols.

Sit back for a moment. Contemplate: If you were King, how would you order your private life?

- How would your staff address you?
- How would your staff take care of you?
- When guests come for dinner, how would you want them to be greeted?
- How would you want guests to be served?
- When you go out in public, who opens doors for you?
- How do you work this out in a multi-slave household?
- When standing around at the mall in a store, how is your slave to be standing?
- Is your slave free to speak to you, or does he/she need to ask permission to speak?

The answers to these, and many more related questions, form the basis of your own protocol manual. In my personal opinion, House Protocols constantly reinforce the uniqueness of the structured M/s Lifestyle. I feel that this area of the M/s dynamic is so important that it became the subject the companion book to this one: <u>Protocol Handbook for the Leather slave: Theory and Practice</u>. To give you a feeling for this topic, I've included a few of my own House Protocols. Bear in mind, every M/s relationship is different; every Master values things slightly differently – you have to work out your own Protocols.

- I am to be addressed as "Master" whenever possible, and as, "Sir" when "Master" would be inappropriate.

- When going out in public – even to the mall – we will always slightly overdress. The slave is to assume the most formal walking and standing protocols possible, without drawing attention to herself (translation: the slave at rest may stand with hands clasped behind her back and resting on her buttocks, rather than locked in the small of her back).

- My slave walks slightly behind my right shoulder and opens all doors for me. In restaurants, I walk to Table ahead of the slave. The slave may not speak to or respond to the wait staff, even if a waiter addresses her and asks her preference in drink or food.

- For meals at home, the slave serves me at Table, then plates her own food and brings it to Table. The slave does not eat until certain ceremonies have been completed.

- The slave will answer the telephone using a prescribed, formal protocol.

House credos can be **vastly** different. Just think how their internal House Protocols would flow from these statements.

- Sir Stephen, International Master 2005, heads a Victorian Household. His protocols, with slave catherine, have been largely recreated out of literature of the Victorian era. Their Household Credo states, in part: "We believe that the Household of Sir Stephen has a responsibility to itself and its members to fulfill those needs for which we have come together. To find the fulfillment we seek in giving and receiving superior service. Further, and as important, we have a responsibility to the larger Master/slave community to act in harmony with other Households and to strive, always, to promote greater harmony within that community." (Taken from their website: www.restraining-order.com)

- Master Alex Keppeler, head of Household Keppeler,

writes of his spiritually-based Household: "We believe that our life in leather is a journey of self-knowledge and self-discovery in which one hopes to discover how he relates to The Other, to himself, to others in the Household and to the outside world. We are not isolated in our vision, but seek to draw on historical sources of the leather tradition and the communal aspects of the Rule of St. Benedict, and on the resources of others who are treading a similar path." (Taken from his website: www.householdk.org)

Again, an M/s relationship is special. It is *structured.* Some actions are prescribed (required); other actions are proscribed (forbidden).

Expectations Governing Family Behavior

The "feel" of your House is set by your key values. Your values are made real through your choice of protocols. Your protocols are an expression of your expectations.

As Master, you are expected clearly to specify your expectations about your slave's behavior, both in public and in private. There are many ways of approaching this – here are a few ideas that I use in my Family:

- I expect my slave to live and to serve me *effortlessly technique.* In my Household, everything is to look effortless; meals are to come together on time and perfectly.

- I expect my slave to support our intention that every day is magical and special. In this light, my slave is to maintain the house to the point that it is always tidy, and that flowers are fresh and nicely arranged.

- I expect my slave to be committed to the road less traveled – to support our quest to gain unusual skills and experiences.

- I expect those associated with this Family to complete any task they begin, and to complete it with excellence.

- I expect those associated with us not to repeat third-hand tales/stories about another person – we recognize that everyone has plenty to work on themselves. Related, I expect those associated with us to behave (and to serve) with grace and elegance in all circumstances.

Once you have identified some of the larger themes by which you wish your House to be known, and once you have spelled out your *expectations* of your Family members, you're ready to take on another large topic: team building. If you think about it for a minute, you probably want your Family to be viewed as a "team" in the business sense of the word. Many of the *rules and guidelines* for building strong teams apply equally to building a strong Family. In summary, they are:

- Be loyal to those not present. Family members will not discuss Family issues with Others. No personal information about Family members will be shared with Others. Parenthetically, if the slave hears someone speaking ill of another, my preference is that the slave urge that person to discuss it directly and constructively with whomever is involved – but not to continue the discussion.

- Don't complain to Others. If any Family member has a concern or complaint about the way the Family is functioning, we will discuss these concerns entirely within the Family – not to friends or Others. Concerns and complaints will receive a better reception if they are presented as facts/issues devoid of emotion and spin. That is, there is an "issue" and there is the "story about the issue." I'm not interested in the story, for it is usually based on personal interpretation.

- Do more than your fair share. I recognize that much is required of my slave. But, that's the nature of the deal. While I'm working very hard to create a magical world filled with intellectual and emotional stimulation, I need my slave to be searching relentlessly for ways of smoothing the way before me.

- Be dependable. Be where you are expected to be at the time you said you would be there; be prepared to do the job-at-hand.

- Anticipate what I am going to do next. Good Family members rarely need to tell one another what to do next, because the partner is already doing it.

- Be flexible. I tend to act quickly once I understand a situation. My slave must be prepared to follow quickly, and without slowing me down. My slave must learn to recognize when I am in problem-solving mode, and learn to interject refining questions at that time – not after I've made a decision.

Expectations About Responsibilities and Duties Inside and Outside the House

What *expectations* do you hold yourself to? What *expectations* do you have of your slave? For example, do you wish to give back to your Leather Community? If so, in what way? I know one Family who goes out of its way to make new submissives feel welcomed and safe. They've set up a "buddy" system, a safe-call system, and monthly introductory-level workshops. I know another Family that advocates for sexual freedom and tolerance between the Vanilla world and the world of BDSM/kink.

Once you start thinking about duties and responsibilities, you may start uncovering previously hidden expectations. For example, you might expect anyone associated with your Family to be *intellectually curious.* You may limit the time they are allowed to spend on *frivolity* – an activity you also get to define. So, in your Household, *no frivolity* might mean restrictions on television and movie viewing. By extension, you might promote intellectually stimulating evenings by offering small (formal) dinner parties. In a similar vein, you might promote reading non-fiction and restrict reading fiction.

The message, then, is that you need seriously to consider what you stand for and how you want to *brand* your Household. And, you need to be open with your slave-to-be about these hidden expectations.

Beliefs – About the Spiritual Side of Life and About People

A substantial proportion of the leaders in the Leather M/s movement discuss the importance of the *spiritual* aspects in their relationships and actions. This represents another topic that, for many, will require serious thought. The spiritual aspect is important for a variety of reasons. For example, it concerns the *purpose* of your SM play. Are you flogging your slave because you like the feeling or the process, or because *flogging* represents a path to spiritual and cathartic release? Think about the slave candidate you're playing with...when you are finished *playing,* does he/she get up and thank you for your skill and technique, or does this person lie there virtually motionless for 20-30 minutes, overwhelmed by the magic that has just enveloped him or her? It's not that one "scene" is inherently better than the other – just that they are *different.* Have you ever thought about BDSM practices as being a *vehicle* to take your partner to a *differnet plane.* Have you ever tried to grapple with what it is the two of you do together that is so *special?*

Let's move now from spiritual beliefs to beliefs about people. It's not important that you agree or disagree with these bulleted points. The issue is: how do you react to these statements that I've collected over the years? By considering which statements elicit emotional responses, you may learn something about yourself. **Let me be clear: these are not my own personal views, just a collection of attitudes that I've heard people express over the years.** It is important that you create and then react to some of your own opinion statements in order to find out how you – and your slave – are wired.

- People? There's nobody out there other than who I create (or recreate) when I go out in the world. Even then, I can only see that person through the filters of my own senses. My "George Washington" is so different from George Washington's "George Washington" that there is not likely to be much common ground beyond a physical description.

- I believe that people are inherently good, kind, and loving. I just have to give them a chance.

- People are only "civilized" out of fear of being caught and exposed. Everyone would rape, murder, and steal, if they thought they could get away with it.

- It is our belief that every person has worth. Even a rapist, con artist, or burglar. You must be able to forgive the person who kills your child.

- If you meet my expectations, I'll like you and let you be my friend. Violate my values one time, and I'll cast you out forever. (This can relate to other concepts such as, honor code or personal values.)

- I believe everyone, until they give me reason not to trust or believe them.

- Thin as a rail; no meat on her/his bones. He/she must be overly controlling and compulsive; no joy in this one – probably an introvert – I'm just not interested.

- Sloppy body, sloppy mind. If the person doesn't care

enough about him/herself to stay thin and trim, I'm just not interested.

- While I can be polite to almost anyone, a person would have to be very special for me to be willing to give of my time or attention. I don't do "normal people" well.

- Gosh, I just love people. Big, tall, short, small. I revel in their alivenes; they all have such interesting stories to tell.

- Son, people have been put on earth to see one another through, not to see through one another.

As you can well imagine, someone who thinks they *recreate people in the world* every time they go out is going to have a dramatically different relationship with people than the person who believes that everyone is inherently good, kind, and loving, or the person who believes that everyone is a rapist at heart.

So, a project: Sit down with your potential partner and work out your beliefs about people. Caveat: you may have trouble actually admitting – or getting your partner to admit – true sentiments on this score. The reason is that if your views are not personally flattering (socially acceptable), you aren't likely to reveal them. Similarly, your partner may be less than honest on this same score.

This, then, forces you back into the world of social science research. You are going to have to work out proxy measures for this topic. Remember: a *proxy measure* is an unrelated – but acceptable – question you can ask that actually answers another question. For example, if you wanted to explore someone's views on self-determination, you might ask some questions about their reactions to street beggars – the homeless.

- How do you think that person got there?

- Do you give money to street people?

- Have you ever considered volunteering at a Salvation Army center or the like?

- Can you imagine ever becoming homeless? Does that frighten you?

- How would you feel about inviting a homeless person to come home with us for a good meal? Well, then how about fixing a nice dinner for someone and driving around until you find the first street person and presenting it to him or her?

- What would you say about spending next weekend doing volunteer service downtown with the XYZ Center?

I suspect that you'll learn a lot about your partner's empathy quotient, while you'll also learn their attitudes about work ethics, cleanliness, fate, and deistic determinism.

Agreements

If you're going to hold someone *accountable,* you have to be sure that they are *aware* of the areas for which they are being held accountable. Over the years, I have come to use structured *agreements* for *things that matter.* I do this because the forced structure of an Agreement makes the communication particularly clear. As I use them, *Agreements* have four components:

- State the offer/acceptance (I agree…).

- Specify the general item to be done (…to wash the outside of the car…).

- List conditions of satisfaction – be clear about the level of activity (…so that all of the dirt and tar are completely removed and no water spots remain…).

- Specify the time frame (…within the next two hours).

If the slave suspects that he/she cannot fully accomplish any of the four aspects of the Agreement, the slave must respectfully decline to agree to it, and then explain the reticence (in our case, I have usually forgotten that my slave is already working on another task and this new task presents a conflict with my own Instructions). The modification of any aspect of the Agreement *must* be done BEFORE the Agreement is accepted or as soon as the need for modification becomes apparent.

If the slave has made an Agreement and later discovers that he/she may be unable to complete it on time, it is VERY IMPORTANT to contact Master and discuss the situation <u>before the time period expires</u>.

Failure to keep an Agreement will carry Consequences.

In my world, Agreements are a big deal. I don't use them casually. I don't mind modifying an agreement at the front end; I don't even mind being contacted regarding a change to the deadline. However, I mind a great deal if no effort was made to renegotiate the terms and conditions of an Agreement, and it is not fulfilled exactly as it was set forth.

Because I am so focused on keeping Agreements perfectly, I caution my slave not to enter lightly into a formal Agreement with me. I'm going to be easier to get along with if the slave says: "Master, with respect, Sir, I cannot fulfill the terms you are proposing, Sir", rather than entering into an Agreement suspecting that the terms cannot be fulfilled.

I will comment further on this point. I've known people who would agree to do just about anything with little or no intention of doing so. I had a professor who would promise anything just to get you to go away. While it seemed that he was being cooperative and helpful, he was simply being manipulative. Aware of my personal sensitivity concerning this point – that I will aggressively challenge any failure to keep an Agreement – I explain *how to manage Agreements* to those who work closely with me. Similarly, on those occasions that I feel an Agreement is needed to accomplish some significant task, I'm careful to review the component parts of the Agreement and remind the slave of the importance of communicating changes to me **ahead of time**.

Time Commitments

In my Household, issues of *time* are important. I view *time* as one of the most valuable assets a person possesses. In life, when you run out of time, you're called *dead.* Since you don't quite know when you will run out of time, every day becomes important. In that sense, I care very much how I spend my time and how my slave spends her time. In addition to the philosophical underpinnings, *time commitments* represent a daily opportunity to keep your word. They are a form of Agreement. If the slave has been told an arrival or departure time, Master expects that time to be honored with precision. There will be Consequences to violating time issues – not the least of which is having to put up with my reaction to the slave being late.

Keeping one's word is a core concept within the Leather culture. From the very beginning of my exposure to the Leather World, I was struck by the degree of honesty, integrity, and high moral purpose I found there. If a Leatherman says something will be done, you can be sure it will be. If I, as Master, have told someone that I will arrive at a certain time, tardiness by my slave will NOT cause me to be late to that meeting. If my slave is not ready to leave on time, I will leave without her and attend to her consequences later.

Chapter Summary

In Part I we discussed some common terms and understandings. In Part II we spent time on self-exploration. Part III was devoted to grappling with key elements of your relationship. This last part – Part IV – focused on the *framework* of your relationship within the larger structure of your Leather House. Now we're ready to tackle the marketing question: how do you find a potential partner? If you're already in a relationship, you may skip on to later parts.

Master/slave Relations

Part V: Finding a slave

This section applies equally to Masters looking for slaves, as to slaves looking for Masters. This is the time that you think through *how* you might want to reach out to such a person and *what* you want a prospective partner to know about you. The hunt for a partner can be extremely casual – almost accidental – or as highly structured as a job search.

This section treats this process more like that of searching for a *job*. This section presumes that you wish to *act* in such a way as to find a slave, rather than to stay cocooned and *dream* of finding a slave.

You may wish to start your search by identifying some *outreach paths*:

- Internet, such as alt.com, slave4master.com, or collarme.com
- Local kink clubs – here are some competent search engines to find kink clubs:
  - www.darkheart.com/usalist.html
  - http://216.166.84.8/a-wwwdir/org.html
  - http://www.drkdesyre.com/meetppl/orgs/orgs.html
  - http://www.leatherpage.com/clubs/clubs.htm
- Weekend kink conferences:
  - http://www.thebdsmeventspage.com/main1.html

Once you have started mingling with like-minded people, the next hurdle concerns *making an appropriate connection* that demon- strates your thorough preparation for a relationship. I would certainly notice it if a petitioning slave came up to me with a card of introduction that gave *just the right amount of information,* and then followed up with a resume such as the one I will describe immediately below. This would communicate his/her clarity of intent, thoughtfulness about details, and what I call, *process.*

Anyway, in my view, **personal marketing** has *components:*

- **Stuff**: how you present yourself
- **Exposure**: where you present yourself
- **Follow-through**: how you keep track of contacts

Stuff – Social Calling Cards, Photos, Resume, Website

In this day-and-age of computer-generated business cards, it's easy and inexpensive for someone with computer skills to print a handful of social calling cards that include a photo. (Note: if you *do* include a photo, then you need bright-white, glossy card-stock. You also may need a photo-quality printer – a few hundred dollars. The image will have to be 300dpi to look good; don't bother trying to print off a 72dpi image. You will need a program like *Adobe Photo Elements*® or *Adobe Photoshop*® to manipulate the image – crop it, lighten or darken it, sharpen it.) Actually, it's likely that the hardest part is getting a competent, uncluttered photo image.

Even a simple social calling card without a photo is better than handing out your work/business card. Your professional business card reveals too much about who you are.

Your Leather/BDSM Master's resume should be contained on a single page, and should include topics such as:

- Who you are – scene name or real name, but not address. Marital status.

- Means of contact – cell phone? E-mail? Through a website?

- What you seek – skills, talents, capabilities, duration. Are you looking for a play partner, a third, a weekend event or a 24/7 relationship?

- What you like – your particular kink(s).

- What you seek – the "ideal slave" kind of thing.

- Your Leather history – are you part of a local group? Do you go to regional conferences?

- Accomplishments – do you speak at BDSM events? Are you recognized for mastery in some BDSM arena?

- General overview of your education and work experiences.

- Hobbies/interests?

- Etc.

Next, I suggest that you consider preparing a set of questions that you would ask your potential slave or Master. You can build these from our earlier sections, or simply sit down and start thinking of things you would like to know about this person. Everyone's list would be somewhat different, but here's a start...

- In what areas of life do you consider yourself truly accomplished?

- Have you been particularly successful in your work life? Tell me about that.

- How do you make your money grow?

- Tell me about your relations with your prior spouse(s) and children. Are you close with your family? What about your parents and siblings?

- What areas do you hope to explore in the next five years?

- Conceptually, what do you think of playing by SSC (Safe, Sane and Consensual) rules? In your view, what are the strengths and weaknesses of using SSC rules vs. RACK (Risk-Aware Consensual Kink) standards?

- What leisure-time activities do you enjoy?
- What first comes to mind when you see a street person begging for money?
- Tell me something of your spirituality.
- Do you smoke? Drink? Use recreational drugs?
- Do you enjoy meeting new people? How do you do this? If not, why not?
- What volunteer work have you done in the past?
- What are your favorite TV shows? Movies? Books?
- How would you describe your spirit of adventure.
- What's your Leather history?
- Ever tried a polyamorous or swinging lifestyle? When were you last tested for STDs and what were the results? What's your position on condom use?
- Do you have lots of friends? Where do you go to be with them? What kind of activities do you do with them?
- What specific BDSM skills do you have? CBT? Flogging?
- What specific BDSM play do you particularly enjoy or particularly avoid?

These are proxy questions for key issues about kindness, loyalty, personal competence, self-confidence, personal ethics, kink preferences, self-reliance, and so forth. They are only part of your packet of questions. It is up to you to extend this list.

The next group of questions concern what your *slave candidate* may be seeking. Again, you really need to think this list through and create one that comes from YOUR being, not from my head. Consider the next two lists as starting points.

Questions a Master Might Ask of a submissive/slave

- Don't get me wrong, I'm flattered, but why did you pick ME to petition?

- Specifically, what skills do you seek in a Master? What evidence do you have that I can help you with that?

- Name some life-goals that you think I could help you attain.

- How do you see me helping you grow in personal or skill areas?

- How have you prepared to be a slave? Have you been in service before? (NOTE: it is very important that you learn about this person from others within his or her community. See below for the section on "Poor Quality submissive/slave.")

- "Living in Service" can mean different things to different people; can you explain what living in service means to you?

- What acts of service have you experienced – both for pay and as a volunteer?

- There's a lot of discussion about loving your slave. Where do you stand on the subject of love in M/s relations?

- In your past relationships, how have prior Masters distinguished between punishment and correction? Please give examples of a few issues that occurred to you that you suspect would cause me to punish or to correct you.

- What kinds of support/help do you seek from a Master?

What role do you wish your Master to fulfill?

- Are there times in your past relationships when you were loaned out? Tell me about those. What was the purpose in loaning you out, and how did you feel about that? What safeguards were in place when you were loaned out? Did you feel those were adequate?

- Please describe in detail the kind of sex play you particularly enjoy. Said differently, what level of sex play do you wish of me? What experiences have you had with a polyamorous lifestyle? (If you, the reader, are also interested in the swinging lifestyle, you will have to develop appropriate questions.)

- In the future, I might wish to consider having more than one slave. How do you react to that?

- In your prior M/s relationships, how was SM play folded in with daily living?

Do you already have a website? If it's not appropriate to use your existing website to promote your search for a slave, perhaps you could have another site built for that purpose. A decision to build a website to advertise your search for a slave is highly individual and depends not only on *who you are,* but also the degree to which you are used to having a web presence.

Exposure: Presentation and Follow-Through

Okay, let's presume that you've prepared your bio and thought through questions to ask a prospective respondent; you've prepared all this *stuff,* now what? Well, you can *advertise.*

- Local e-groups
- Alt.com; bondage.com; collarme.com; slave4master. com and similar websites
- Personals sections of newspapers
- Local munches and meetings

But advertising, alone, may not be enough. Depending upon the extent of the response, you may need to develop a way to keep track of the contacts. This doesn't have to be elaborate, but it's a matter of making notes of what you did/said to the person so you don't get the people confused. (I can hear you already: "How confused can I get with zero responses?") Take heart. You're fishing in a really, really small pond. Think about it. There's the total U.S. population. Then there is the subpopulation of people who are kinky. Within that, the subpopulation of those who are interested in power exchange. Within that, those who are interested in a *structured relationship* – Master/slave relations. Small group. A few thousand couples in the U.S.? Regional conferences get about 200 people. They're expensive, yes, but people practicing this Lifestyle are pretty passionate about it and may show up at M/s conferences in greater percentages than for general BDSM conferences.

The point is, you may find it's hard to find a good match. I've watched both Doms and subs in my local Community hunt and hunt and hunt. Ultimately, I've suggested to more than one person that they start writing articles and books in order to become known and to gain access to a wider pool of candidates.

Some Special Considerations if You or Your slave are New to the Lifestyle

If your slave is new to the Lifestyle – and if YOU are fairly new to the Lifestyle – your greatest risk is probably in scaring him/her. I have a friend – a Leatherwoman who had been in the Lifestyle for one year – who took a fairly new-to-the-lifestyle date to a *dark party* (a no-rules party), and was upset that he didn't know how to behave. Are we surprised, here?

I have another friend who was so excited about finally collaring his slave, that he ordered her to wear the collar to work. Not a good idea; this collar wasn't very discreet. Soon, the slave was embroiled at work in one minor controversy after another. The slave never lost her job, but she had the sense that she was monitored much more closely, and *differently,* than her peers.

Message: it's going to take some time for those new to this sub-culture – whether new as a Master or new as a slave – to learn how to behave and act separately and together in ways that don't cause others to roll their eyes. How many times have we heard stories of Internet Doms showing up at a public play party and causing an uproar by grabbing someone's slave/submissive by the collar? How many times have we heard about the new person walking right across an ongoing scene? How many times have we watched with some mixture of horror and fascination as a new-to-real-life Dom would sit down beside someone's collared slave and start talking to her?

Anyway, the reality is that we all started out at the beginning, and once we've been submerged in this Lifestyle for some years, we tend to forget how different we are now from the person we were then. Don't overwhelm your new slave candidate.

Getting to Know You; Getting to Know All About You

Before you begin a relationship, I **strongly** recommend getting to know the person in a very Vanilla way. In the opening stages of your relationship, you – as Master – should be sharing equal psychological power and authority with your slave candidate. So, take some time with this person in order to figure out how they act and react to unusual situations. Try spending a weekend in a single bed. Make up some reason why it has to be this way, and consider the reactions. Take your slave candidate out slumming for dinner one night, and then have him/her get seriously dressed up another night. See how you guys behave for a weekend at a four-star hotel, then at a dive. Who is doing the fussing, and what are they fussing about?

I've had any number of instances where my own prejudices rushed to the surface and danced on my head giggling, as I watched someone who certainly didn't *look* the part, exhibit extremely refined manners and behaviors. Similarly, I've had a few experiences where a drop-dead gorgeous and immaculately coiffed Thing shattered the spell, which then crashed to the ground, flopping and gasping for breath. She had opened her mouth and *said something* that came out in non-grammatical English. But, these are **my** hang-ups and not yours. You get to be honest and derive your own self-truths.

So, I suggest you start with a short contract; three months seems to be common (it follows, shortly). Also, the Internet contains many contract examples, although they are of varying degrees of utility. In my own life, I offered my slave a three-month contract and renewed it twice before moving to a year-long contract that covered a period that she was under *consideration* for the permanent collar that I ultimately offered her.

Guarding Against a Poor Quality submissive/slave

As a Master, you may find that you've become entangled with an out-of-control slave who talks about you behind your back. It may take some time for you to realize this is going on. Some defenses – particularly relating to established submissives:

- Ask your potential slave to provide references. References that you already know. This may be somewhat round-about, but it can be done. Person "X" knows person "Y," who knows person "Z," whom you also know. Ours is a pretty small Community.

- Do some additional research. Learn something about the person you are considering taking on as a slave. Listen for what you are NOT being told, as well as what you ARE being told. Listen for unusual phrasing: "Oh, gosh, sure I know lovelybod. Oh, I don't think it's appropriate for me to say anything about her – that would sound too much like gossip, you know what I mean?"

Because our Community so relies on *personal endorsements,* it's *extremely important* that you couldn't get one for lovelybod. Your follow-up question might be: "Oh, can you give me the name of anyone who *could* give me an endorsement?" If your source now says something like: "Oh, gosh, that would really be hard. I just don't know...", you know that you've just unfurled a big red flag.

- Attend your local kink meeting with your potential slave. How does he/she behave? Is he/she welcomed like a person of high value, or like some gruesome plague? Does this person appear to be surrounded by a closed circle of friends (a clique?), or does this person mix with the general assembly? In fact, what conclusions can you draw about this person by the others with whom he/she meets?

Serious Warning Flags About a Person

Everyone is human. We all have foibles and follies. But, if you've run into someone who is exhibiting a number of the following traits, chances are that person is *miserable* with him or herself. Someone who is personally miserable is really likely to make YOU miserable. So tread carefully.

- Uses "I" as often as possible
- Is sensitive to (perceived) slights by others
- Is jealous and envious
- Thinks only of him/herself
- Talks mainly of him/herself
- Trusts no one
- Never forgets a criticism
- Always expects to be appreciated, always fishing for compliments

- Is suspicious of the intentions of others
- Listens greedily to what others say of him/her
- Always mentions faults in others
- Does as little as possible for others
- Shirks duties, if possible
- Never forgets a service he/she may have rendered to someone
- Sulks if people aren't grateful for his/her favors
- Demands agreement with his/her own views on everything
- Only looks for a good time
- Loves him/herself first
- Is selfish, if at all possible

So, when it comes to searching for a slave, remember the aphorism: *When you don't know what to do, do it slowly.*

Chapter Summary

This chapter focused on *finding a slave.* I gave you some Internet links to help you find local kink clubs and a link to help you locate weekend kink conferences. I suggested you consider making up some non-business kinky calling cards, prepare a Master's Resume, and consider creating a website to promote your search for a slave. I supplied a series of questions that a Master might ask a slave candidate and offered some suggestions about guarding yourself against a poor quality submissive. I ended with a bulleted list of potential *red flags* about a person you're considering for an intimate slave.

Now, we're ready to move to the next chapter – *beginning a relationship.*

"It's not what you think about the relationship, it's how you think about the relationship."

Master Jim Glass,
Northeast Master/slave Conference, 2006

Part VI: Beginning a Relationship

When I attend Master/slave conferences, I'm struck by the fact that most of these relationships are among *older people* – 40+. Quite a population is over 55. This tells me a few things. First, this kind of *structured relationship* may appeal more to people who have been married once or twice; and second, *personal maturity* also helps.

Because a Master/slave relationship is **still** a form of relationship – and holds the potential for excitement and fulfillment – people sometimes let down their guard in the hopes that if they just over-look this or that little difficulty, the fit will be *close enough* to work out. That's probably not a great idea.

CPR – the *Core Truth* about an M/s Relationship

As Master Jim Glass points out, a Master/slave relationship is about **CPR**: *Control* plus *Power* produces *Respect.* As I've commented previously, your slave is not your boyfriend or girl-friend. This is *not* a vanilla relationship. As Master, you must master both the verbal and non-verbal techniques of exuding personal power.

But, how do you exude *personal power* if it does not come natu-rally to you? Where does the *control* come from? An Internet search may be helpful, but here are some bulleted notes.

Tips on developing *command presence*:
- Give a good first impression – every day. You don't want to look like an unmade bed.
  - Always wear clean, pressed clothing; dress profes-

sionally.

- Is your car clean, inside and out?
- If you work in an office, keep it extremely clean and tidy.

- Be conscious of your physical stance.
  - Legs apart, shoulder width.
  - Hands to sides, NOT in front or in back.
  - Be careful to be *planted* and not to rock or sway.
  - Don't *lean* on anything.

- Attend to how you *walk*. How you carry yourself portrays command presence or lack of it. Confidence is projected through your body language and how you verbally deal with individuals and groups.
  - Walk with intent. Don't shuffle your feet or use a "lazy" walk. Pick up your feet and move like you know where you are going and that you have a purpose in going there.
  - Walk with your head up, eyes alert, and your expression intent. You do not want to appear weak or vulnerable. You want to project the image of someone who knows why they are where they are, and who is trained and knows what they are doing.
  - Portray an "I am in charge of this situation" image. The key is to be *outwardly confident* – even if on the inside you are scared out of your wits. You want your body language to convey confidence.

- Attend to how you *speak*.
  - Your speech is another aspect of command presence. *More people than you think hear you speak.*
  - Don't say too much – when you're silent, people take it to mean you're "deep."
  - Don't say anything that you don't have to say – *knowledge is power:* don't give it away.

An M/s Studies Book

- ◦ If you make a mistake, apologize and clean up your own mess. You are responsible for ensuring that your message is heard the way you intended.
- ◦ Use a strong, well-modulated voice (practice being forceful with yourself in a mirror – preferably naked). (I knew a female police lieutenant who said she taught herself voice control by forcefully instructing a chair to remain just where it was. She went on to be an instructor in *command presence* at a police academy.)
- • If someone was watching you to see how you reacted if they did something wrong, what would they think?
  - ◦ How do you sit, stand, and walk when at work?
  - ◦ Do you walk around with your hands in your pockets?
  - ◦ Do you look at the ground all the time?
  - ◦ Do you look bored and inattentive? Monitor yourself; practice being assertive without being domineering. Keeping your cool is also a big part of this.

Command presence boils down to how you present yourself. Do you "look the part?" Do you carry yourself with confidence? Do you ACT the part? Do you speak the part? If you can, then you are developing Command Presence, which will make your job as Master a LOT easier.

Starting a New Relationship – a Period of Being Crazy

For many people, the first several months of a new relationship are characterized by a wild emotional high. The new partner is heaven-sent. The new partner is the most amazing surprise you've ever had. The new partner does everything perfectly. The new partner is so smart, talented, wise. The new partner, the new partner, the new partner. Jay Wiseman tells me that in polyamorous circles, this is known NRE – New Relationship Energy.

That's why most Seniors that you ask, will advise you to **slow down**. Take it easy. Don't rush. Get to know the person as a person. That's why training contracts are often 3-4 months long. You have to see how the new partner looks and behaves in **six** months.

Some Early Indications of Problems with Your New slave

In our Community, there are some early warning signs of trouble:

- Your new slave has accepted this relationship with you, but has NOT checked YOUR reputation within your local Community. If your potential slave hasn't checked you out, they are either unusually naïve, an unsafe player, or may be so inexperienced that they don't know how to check you out. Or they may be a little arrogant and feel that they can discern all your strengths and weaknesses on their own. This is not likely to be true, is it?

- Your new slave may be addicted to drugs, alcohol, sex, pain, food, etc. This can be pretty self-evident. But, people with active or prior addictions have certain common characteristics that can include stunted emotional development – so, you may wish to do some research into "addictive behavior" before getting too heavily involved.

- Your new slave won't account for a block of time that has disappeared. He/she keeps ducking and weaving when asked the simple question: "Where were you?" (Warning: she/he may have been out finding you a surprise birthday present – so, be careful about forcing an answer.) Your new slave has frequent personal crises beyond the normal or average that could be expected in any life. This could indicate that this person may – through their personal choices – bring these problems upon themselves. I doubt that you will enjoy being along for that ride.

- Your new slave seems to have dramatic mood swings: nice and pleasant most of the time, then aggressive and abusive without warning. Same comment as above: this is not normal and you will probably not enjoy being along for that ride.

General Warning Flags Concerning submissives/slaves

- **Passive/aggressive behavior:** He/she keeps saying "yes", yet your request is utterly ignored or poorly completed. Outward behaviors such as these have deep roots. It's not likely you will be able to do something with a fully grown adult who exhibits them.

- **Secretive behavior:** The slave keeps an online journal (blog) that you either don't know about or don't monitor on the grounds that it is trivial. (I know of a case where a Dom chose not to monitor his submissive's blog. As it happened, she was a distrubed person and was broadcasting extremely private and negative half-truths about him. These unchallenged fabrications went around the "submssives network" like wildfire and caused him to be declared *persona non grata* in a number of local clubs.)

- **Warnings from others:** People seem to be trying to tell you something about your slave candidate, but you can't quite understand what they're getting at. You sense that you're being offered a warning, but you bristle, and the other person retreats. All I can say to this is: suppress your knee-jerk defense of the slave candidate and listen.

- **Refusal to negotiate:** Your slave-to-be doesn't want to have a formal negotiation and contract with you on the grounds that this is a Master/slave relationship, and as Master, you surely know how to treat him/her, and you only need to know that he/she wants to serve you. Ummmm, errrrr this is, perhaps, an Internet person? Knowing, understanding, and communicating your limits and needs will help prevent abuses of trust.

So, let's say that NO *red flags* have surfaced. As the Master, you are ready to start negotiating the terms and conditions of your relationship. That means a **contract.** There are mixed feelings about contracts, so let me take a minute and share my thoughts.

Negotiations

The next few pages are about negotiating about the ownership and use of your slave's body.

Heady stuff.

For starters, if you've not done a fair amount of negotiation in your life, you'll want to read these sections more than once. Also, if you're negotiating with an intended slave who has not negotiated a number of prior contracts, moral/ethical honor binds you to recommend to your intended that he/she seek an experienced Master to represent him/her in negotiations with YOU.

Opening Notes
In real-life business negotiations, it is a truism that the *real guts of the negotiation occur just as the clock is running out.* That is, if you allow an hour for a negotiation, most of the serious issues get negotiated in the last five minutes. If you allow a day, they

get negotiated in the last five minutes. If you allow a week, they get negotiated in the last five minutes.

Also, you will be able to conclude a much more successful negotiation if you understand your slave's needs/wants through his/her eyes. The better you understand what the *other person* **needs** vs. **wants**, the cleaner and clearer the negotiation. That said, I'll now start in on this section.

———————————————

Much is said about negotiations. *Negotiations* live in the world of D/s (for scening) and M/s (for the first few years of the relationship, at any rate). On a strictly logical level, it's hard to imagine a slave negotiating for any "rights," but that discussion should be saved for the *advanced* class.

My own experience is that slaveless Masters often jump right in to "negotiations" with slave candidates before taking the time to learn about the **PERSON** who is petitioning to be the slave. I certainly endorse the use of short-term contracts that provide some minimal guidance for both parties while the two people endeavor to learn about one another. **NOTE: I caution you against drafting an initial training contract that exposes your intended slave to the full brunt of your idiosyncrasies and protocols.**

- Consider putting yourself and your intended slave through a series of personality and skill-battery tests. At a minimum, an online IQ test and a Meyers-Briggs test; ideally, find some tests that will demonstrate both your preferred working styles and your mutual skills.

- Consider taking courses/workshops that promote a common set of problem solving skills – Landmark Education comes to mind.

About Negotiating

- We negotiate all the time.

- Almost everything is negotiable.

- Avoid early positions.

- First, create value. Why should someone want you or what you are offering?

- The first option isn't necessarily the best. Create many options.

- Deadlines can be tricky when you're negotiating matters of the heart. However, in business negotiations, the general rule is to negotiate early, or to use deadlines to achieve success.

- "No" means "no" when dealing with sexual issues. However, you may sometimes treat "no" as "not yet" if you're negotiating a service issue. Often "no" simply indicates that you haven't explained the benefits in terms that appeal to your listener.

- While the textbook on tough negotiations instructs you to give concessions only when you get something in return, you might consider introducing humorous concessions when you negotiate your M/s contract. That is, if Master wants the floors scrubbed each Saturday morning, the concession could be that Master takes his slave out to dinner each Saturday night.

- Use: "What if..." to break open the discussion to create value.

- You must leave the other person with a sense of satisfaction. This is the "win/win" school of negotiation, not the "winner takes all" school.

- Do your homework. Determine your partner's "below-the-surface" needs. Determine *why* your intended slave is seeking certain specific terms or conditions.

- Take the other person INTO THE FUTURE to see possible results of various positions.

Problems with Negotiations – YOU as the Buyer

Some negotiations go better than others, yes? Sometimes you come away feeling really good about the outcome, but sometimes you feel that the other person got more than you did. Here are some reasons.

Disparity of power:

- You may be exhibiting – or you may be negotiating with someone exhibiting – *Alpha male* characteristics – pushy and assertive/aggressive. Apart from having to decide if you want this kind of personality in your life, you may find it nearly impossible to be *heard.* That's a problem.

- Your opposite (either the Master looking for the slave or the slave looking for the Master) may need to sell themselves to you more than you need to add them to your life.

Disparity of information:

- Your opposite may have done much more research on you than you did on him/her.

- Your opposite may be *much more experienced* in M/s relations than you, and may **assume** that you know/ understand things that never even occurred to you.

- The other person may specifically be *hiding things from you.*

- Your opposite may know that he/she has another candidate in the wings if you don't work out. In the alternative, they may know YOU have another candidate waiting, if they don't work out.

Disparity of experience:

- You may have this kind of interview/negotiation all the time; your opposite may do it only once or twice a year. This is particularly true of Doms/Dommes who may be (culturally) more used to being the negotiators in relationships, and also of Doms/Dommes who may be more used to interviewing or negotiating with subs for BDSM scenes or for relationship positions.

- Your slave candidate may not be used to thinking like a salesman, yet the success of this negotiation depends upon each of your selling points.

Disparity of pressure:

- Is your opposite a "high-value slave?" That is, if you don't compromise and agree to his/her terms, is there another person waiting to accept those terms?

- Are you rushing in to replace a relationship that just ended? Are you under social or personal pressure to demonstrate that you're OK and the proof is that you can immediately form another relationship?

WHAT do You Negotiate?

Remember: this is a book about Master/slave relationships, not Owner/slave relationships. In that light, it is still relevant to discuss *negotiating the relationship.* Also, bear in mind that I'm assuming that you are going to start out with a *training contract,* and not a full-blown M/s contract – for that is hugely different. This is the *getting-to-know-you* stage, not the *okay, here we go* stage.

In a general way, I suggest you, as Master, negotiate the *indicators of success for the next three months.* Note: the points I'll mention here live outside the "boilerplate" language of a contract. I'll assume that your slave candidate will agree to serve you with humility and to please you in a variety of ways, and so forth. These comments go beyond those statements/actions:

- If you're going to require the slave to be studying, how much time does that involve per day or week?

- If the slave is going to be journaling, what is the content of the entries and how long must they be? (NOTE: I failed to negotiate this with my slave, and, as a result, she thought that sending me summaries of her day fulfilled her journaling obligations. I was looking for introspection and didn't care very much about what she did at work during the day. As a result, we were both disappointed about the journaling experience: she was hurt that I didn't respond to her writing; I was disappointed that I wasn't getting any "meat" out of the exercise.)

- If you are going to allow your slave to retain certain rights, be crystal clear about that.

- During this trial period, you may want total and solitary sexual access to your slave. But, there are many combinations out there. I know of a case where the slave is owned by someone who wanted to take her to swinging parties – and that had to be negotiated up front. I know another case where a woman had her own vanilla lover of many years before becoming a slave to another man.

- Staying on the sexual front for a minute, will you, as Master, require the slave to stop all self-pleasuring during this period? And what if Master considers "self-pleasuring" to include eating chocolate? Again, be specific.

- How much full responsibility are you agreeing to take on during this opening period? What if...
  - The slave is fired from work five weeks into the relationship and can't make his/her rent payment? Do you take over?
  - The slave is out running an errand for you and is injured in a car accident; what is your moral/ethical position? What if it's YOUR car?
  - You are playing with your slave and you hit a *land mine* that triggers a psychotic episode in your slave; he/she requires long-term therapy. What's

your moral/ethical position in *this* case?

- If you wish your slave to dress in a certain way, who's paying for the outfits during the trial period? Will you pay for the first $500 of outfits? The first $200 or $1,500? (You may think I'm pulling this stuff out of thin air – I'm not. My fetish involves dressing elaborately for full fetish formal dinners. We do this many times a week. For me, a slave's appeal is affected by how she looks when *all dressed up*. Dressing this way extends to manicures, pedicures, and shoe choice, as well as hair and makeup combinations.)

- What if **you** are an experienced player, but **your slave** is fairly new to the Lifestyle: are you still going to negotiate playing by RACK standards (Risk Aware Consensual Kink - a more advanced form of play), or are you going to go back to SSC standards (Safe, Sane and Consensual)? Does your slave understand the differences? (If you are not familiar with the crucial differences between these sets of rules for BDSM play, please seek out an experienced kinkster and go out for a cup of coffee to discuss it.)

- If you are requiring a *full disclosure contract*, does your slave candidate fully understand exactly what you mean by that phrase? You may want to explain clearly that this will mean that you can rightfully demand to know from your slave **anything** that another person says to him/her "in confidence." Further, you should explain that your slave will be bound to volunteer that information to you if, in his/her heart-of-hearts, the slave knows that Master would like to know about it. Jay Wiseman points out that this creates a seperate duty on the slaves part to tell someone *in advance* that nothing said to this slave can be held "in confidence."

Too much work? Think you can bypass some of this minutiae?

Maybe, maybe not. Did you ever consider what could happen if you *don't* go through a thorough negotiation process? Let me help you with a real answer that concurrently provides some comic relief. Seen this one, lately? It's called *The Etiology of a Crisis.* I've added the M/s storyline.

- **Wild Enthusiasm:** (Ohmygosh, I finally found some-

Leadership is intangible, hard to measure, and difficult to describe. Its quality would stem from many factors. Self-confidence based on expert knowledge, initiative, loyalty, pride, and a sense of responsibility. They are not easily learned. But leaders can be and are made.

General C.B. Cates, 19th Commandant of the USMC

---

one willing to be my slave!!)

- **Disillusionment:** (Ohmygosh, this person is not such a good fit; how could I have done this???)

- **Total Confusion:** (Ohmygosh, I actually signed a three-month training contract with this person, and my word is my bond, and he/she's making me crazy.)

- **Search for the Guilty:** (This must be her fault. She must have hidden faults from me – everyone knows I'm an excellent judge of people.)

- **Punishment of the Innocent:** (Okay, I'll terminate our contract on the grounds that she won't obey me and then make up some reason why I can excuse myself for treating her as my enemy within the Community.)

- **Promotion of the Uninvolved:** (I'll go over here and take "X" as my new slave. This will show everyone who is watching that there's nothing wrong with ME.)

Okay, quick recap. You're now starting a new relationship. You've decided that this potential slave is OK – no skeletons hiding in the closet. You negotiated your way through a contract and signed it, and now, you're in a structured M/s Relationship.

Good work. But, let me talk only to Master for a few pages.

How do You Empower Your Family?

Pardon my presumption, but I assume that if you've gone to all the trouble to create as unusual a relationship structure as this, you want something really special to result. I would argue that to successfully build an *Empowered Family* – whether locally or remotely – you should consider the following:

- You must create a shared sense of purpose. I've already discussed how a Leather Household has its own characteristics and how the House becomes known for its attributes. In that light, it's critical that both of you can articulate those House Values and that all the members of your Household share your big picture. Your leadership job is to ensure that individual Family members feel as though they're contributing to this larger effort.

- You must develop procedures that ensure shared decision-making. Boy, can I hear the howls of derision on this one! Okay, let me frame it. Master is responsible for ensuring that all Household members feel that their thoughts and actions are important to the Family's success. That is: everyone in the Family needs to know that the leader (and possibly other Family members) values their contributions. Yes, Master makes the final decision; but – in reality – that decision will be more fully embraced when all Family members see their suggestions honored and applied to the final resolution. Remember, while you may be the King in a benevolent monarchy; you're not going to last long as a dictator: this is a consensual relationship.

- You must build expected norms for behavior. Family members must understand explicitly what they can expect from one another in terms of communication, support and respect. In our world, this is called a *Protocol Manual,* and is the subject of my companion book, <u>Protocol Handbook for the Leather slave: Theory and Practice</u>. They must know what they will and will not tolerate from one another. When norms are clear, Family members can work together rapidly and correct mistakes rapidly, because they trust one another.

How do You Solve Problems?

I used to work for the U.S. Department of Justice's Law Enforcement Assistance Administration. We had a joke in our division that ran like this: If your problem is that you don't think you have a problem, then you have a problem.

In interpersonal relationships, one party often fails to see a problem that is crystal clear to any outsider. So, I'm going to take some time to discuss ways to identify and solve problems. First, let's start with how you even identify a problem.

In a broad way, there are two kinds of problems. There are problems figuring out **how to do something,** and there are problems with **people performing some act/function.** I will tackle solutions/approaches to each kind of problem.

The material in the first part of this section is really, really helpful, as long as the problem you're about to tackle has to do with a desire to move the Family dynamic from one set of conditions to another set of conditions.

1. **Frame the issues:**
   Understand/explicate the problem. Often the *real* problem is to be able to describe the *core issue(s)* that are begging

for solutions.

For example, it may help you to distinguish whether you have a HARD or a SOFT problem. That is, you have to identify the *kind of issue* that you're confronting.

- **HARD problems** are issues to which you have to **react**. They are "givens." They are those conditions over which you have very little control. For example, they could involve your Family's relations in the context of the community or part of the country in which you live. Another *hard issue* would be the social acceptability of your lifestyle in the context of the city, county or state in which you live. In the business world, *hard problems* concern such things as the political leadership out of Washington, laws, market constraints, product manufacturing, etc. Legal or health care issues sometimes arise that may have a bearing on where you reside.

- **SOFT problems**, then, are those over which you *do* have quite a bit of choice and control. For example, whether or not you speak French is a *soft problem* because you can alter the answer by taking courses that teach you to speak French. Similarly, getting *more education* or gaining *additional skills* are both **soft problems.**

2. **Amplify the problem;** get better data – whether a hard or a soft problem:
   - Who **says** it's a problem? Who wants it fixed?
   - **How** do you measure this problem?
   - **What is** that measurement now?
   - What do you want that measurement to be **now and over time?**
   - What is the **value to your Family of the difference** between what it is now and what you want it to be?
   - **Who** or **what else** is affected?

3. **Create a list of the kinds of results** you would like to

see for each of these problems. This becomes part of the goal-setting process. The relevant aphorism is: *"What gets written down gets done."* The key is to concentrate on the effects of the problem, not on the problem, itself.

4. **Build a new range of options** for introducing the idea into your Family.

Wisdom has two parts: Having a lot to say, and not saying it.

---

5. **Build support** for your idea.
6. **Make distinctions:**
   - Perceived problem vs. the "real" problem
   - Accepted problem vs. underlying causes/issues
   - Political expediency vs. tough alternatives

Exercises such as this can help to strengthen your M/s relationship by bringing *clarity* to the larger issues that surround your relationship, or by clarifying issues that you think may inhibit your relationship from growing or moving into other dimensions. For example, you may fear/assume that some external force or condition is somehow limiting you or your Family. Discussing it and mapping the dimensions of the situation is likely to reveal some heretofore hidden options and opportunities.

The second part of this section concerns **performance problems.** This is the section you want to consider if your problem concerns your slave's behavior in some way. My all-time favorite book for teasing apart *performance problems* is <u>Analyzing Performance Problems: Or, You Really Oughta Wanna – How to Figure out Why People Aren't Doing What They Should Be, and What to do About It</u>, by Robert Mager and Peter Pipe. About the best I can do, here, is to reproduce part of their table of contents – as I so strongly recommend you purchase the book.

I want to start this section with an admonition. If you think your problem deals with the performance of your slave, consider this…

Often, the problem with performance problems is that they are not what they at first appear to be. Not by a long shot. The slave's failure to do "X" *really means* "Y"…, or "K" or "B". What it *really* means may not be easily or logically derived. The slave may not be doing "X" because of an emotional hurt that will take some probing to reveal. That said, here is a start at a structure for teasing the situation apart.

Remember, this material comes from the table of contents of the Mager and Pipe book (tailored to the subject matter of this book, of course).

1. **Is your slave not doing what he/she should be doing?**

   - What is the performance discrepancy? (Quantify the problem; explain to your slave why you care about this.)

   - Specifically, how does the problem manifest itself now?

   - How long has it been a problem?

   - Who is affected and why do they care?

   - How will you know if you're successful in fixing it?

   - Is it worth pursuing? Some issues don't rise to the level of "problems." Some issues are simply not worth addressing when they first surface. Personally, I will sometimes wait quite a while for the correct conditions to arise before discussing a behavior that I want modified. It's not that I'm *hiding a problem;* it's that the particular issue isn't worth addressing at that time.

     Let me speak for a minute on what is called *approximated behavior.* For our purposes, "approximated behavior" is behavior exhibited by your slave that is *on the right path* to being the behavior you seek, but not the *exact, precise* behavior you seek. Because your slave has to learn quite a bit of new behavior in order to mesh successfully and seamlessly with your life, you are bound to go through a period where little things *just aren't quite right.* Here, you have two choices:

- Keep picking on the "little issues."
- Ignore the "little issues."

The problem with picking on them is that you risk pissing off your slave and giving him/her the idea that you are unreasonably (compulsively) picky. The other alternative is to say to yourself, as Master: "Look, I've accepted this person as my slave, and this is what I have to work with right now. Let me cherish this slave while he/she learns all my preferences and protocols. As the slave masters one set of duties/functions, I'll just add another set – *incrementally.*" The key to making this work for you will be to set clear **priorities** with your slave about those preferences and protocols that you want mastered first, and then those that can be mastered later.

2. **Explore fast fixes** – there are likely to be some quick ways to solve the problem right away. Examples include:
   - Explain the rule or the procedure more clearly.
   - Change or eliminate the rule.

3. **Are the consequences for the desired behavior *right side up?***

   - Is the desired performance *itself* punishing? (It takes much longer to do it right.)

   - Is the undesired performance rewarding? (It's simply easier not to mop the kitchen floor every night. The slave gets more time with you.)

- Are there any *consequences* at all? (This is a test of your Mastery and your commitment to the M/s relationship. As Master, you may choose to instruct your slave to leave certain evening tasks incomplete in order that the two of you can *play*. The key, though, lies in the consciousness of the choice. That is, there is a **VAST** difference between **the slave** simply leaving the evening dishes undone in order to be available to play with you, and **you instructing the slave** to leave the dishes undone in order to come and play with you. In the first instance, the slave appears to have acted willfully – making the decision to leave the dishes undone – rather than acting per your instruction.)

4. **Are there other causes for the undesired behavior?**

   - Is the problem a skill deficiency?
   - Could your slave perform this task in the past?
   - Is this skill used often?
   - Can the task be simplified?
   - Are there obstacles remaining? (Outmoded equipment, lack of funds to buy something?)
   - Is the slave properly motivated to complete the task to your specifications?

Again, I urge you to purchase the book Analyzing Performance Problems – I consider it a *core reading* for someone concerned with Master/slave relations.

Chapter Summary

We've now worked ourselves through the chapter on beginning a relationship. I opened with a section covering some indications that everything might not be running smoothly in River City. Once past this point, I ran through some of the salient points about negotiations. What to do and what not to do when negotiating the M/s contract. I discussed how to negotiate by thinking of yourself as the buyer, then reviewed some topics that should be included in any M/s negotiation. Next, I moved on to ways to empower your Family and ways you can approach problem solving. This material should set you up for the next chapter – on contracts and collars.

Master/slave Relations

Part VII: Contracts and Collars

On Contracts

I've heard people dismiss contracts out-of-hand. Their argument is that because it's not possible to make a legally binding contract in the U.S. giving enforceable control over one person to another person, that there is no point to it. I differ. *slave contracts*, while they have no standing in court, are extremely useful to encourage the two (or more) parties to sit down and work through relation-ship issues. Contracts become a way of making a record of what each of you were thinking when you started your relationship.

People tend to forget things; details wash away with time – and age. Contracts don't change their minds. This is not a trivial issue. A clearly worded contract helps prevent needless upsets and recriminations... "But you promised me...", "I never said any such thing..."

Another KEY point: As Joseph Bean likes to point out, your contract is NOT your protocol manual. Your contract is your *constitution.* Your protocol manual would be like a company's by-laws and, like company by-laws, is likely to be changed from time to time. You want to prepare a Contract that is unchanging over time.

In this book, I've included three sample contracts: a training contract, a very detailed long-term contract, and a very short *Owner's contract.* However, before you start reading those, I'd still like to discuss some of the common styles of contracts and some of the more common clauses in contracts of this kind. By now, you probably have one eyebrow cocked and are reflecting on my opening aphorism: *When you don't know what to do, do it slowly.* Yes, this entire process takes a while.

Styles of Contracts

So, let's say you are, in fact, going to prepare a document that specifies the contractual obligations of the partners, better to understand the proposed power exchange relationship. There are three main ways to consider doing this that have worked for other people. I'm sure that there are other ways to do it, but these are the more common ways of approaching contracts in the M/s Lifestyle.

- **Time-controlled contract:** This defines the obligations and duties each will assume at certain points along their agreed path. Normally, the defined level of power exchange starts as a simple structured definition of the relationship at the time. The contract specifies the **furthest** level of power exchange that is comfortable for both parties and explains commensurate duties and obligations. In between are a number of stages, normally between two and four, with each step mapped out. The level of power exchange is normally increased over time, though I am aware of one where the final stage was a required dissolution of the relationship. The timing of when the contractual stages come into force are not usually in the contract. Instead, it is up to the slave to inform the Master that he/she is ready for the next stage (thus giving consent), and for the Master then to inform the slave when the next stage will come into effect (thus retaining control). This type of contract may be most applicable when two people are quite certain at the outset that their relationship will work out, and they know the path along which they wish to travel. While I've never known a couple to use this structure, it seems to me that this can be useful when the Master is much more experienced than the slave, and when he is clear about where he wishes to lead that slave over time.

- **Several contracts used in stages:** This type of contract may be more applicable when two people wish to begin exploring a path together. Here, Master may begin with some kind of temporary contract – perhaps a contract that covers a weekend, or a week or so. This can be viewed as a "getting to know you" contract. It may be fairly brief, but it gives each partner some starting points for developing their relationship. Next, Master may offer a training contract that could last for a number of months, and could, perhaps, be renewed if Master didn't feel the slave had accomplished enough during the first contract period. Next, Master may offer a more extensive contract during a courting period – a period where Master is deciding whether to accept this slave for a lifetime commitment. Finally, Master may offer the slave a much simplified contract for life.

Some notes:
- Each time one contract ends, the NEXT contract is negotiated and prepared, so that both parties know the level of power exchange they must now meet, and also (as with the single time-controlled contract) understand the objective for the next stage, so they can strive to meet it.

- A new *type* of contract is only created once Master is assured that the intent of the previous contract has been fulfilled; that the slave has been able to live within the power and authority structure described in the expiring contract.

- Although it may be hard to accomplish, I strongly suggest that you let one contract expire, and use the next 4-6 weeks to negotiate the next staged contract from a position of *equal personal power*. That is, I urge you NOT to negotiate the next contract from within the M/s relationship. After all, if the slave has given the Master all authority over him/her, how in the world does the slave suddenly have the power to *negotiate???*

- **Single stage (simple) contract**: This contract lays out the core obligations and duties on both sides. This defines the balance of power or authority exchange at the time and leaves open any decrease or increase in that exchange. Typically, these contracts have no ending date. This contract is also known as a No Limits Contract and is usually used in an Owner/slave relationship, rather than a Master/slave relationship.

Common Clauses in Contracts

There are many sample contracts available on the Internet. You may find it hard to identify a pre-existing contract that you could use – without alteration – in your own real-life relationship. That's because people (and their relationships) are so different. At any rate, when drawing up a personal contact, you might want to consider:

- **Health**: The obligations to ensure, or improve, the health of oneself and of the slave. Here, discuss fluid bonding. [NOTE: I recommend that you do NOT include any discussion of weight loss or exercise in your contract. The problem could arise that the slave is unable to exercise for the prescribed number of times or number of hours for whatever reason – even through no fault of his/her own – but he/she has now violated the Contract and is liable for Punishment. It makes much more sense for exercise requirements to be in Instruction or a line or two in your Protocol Manual. Also, dietary and exercise requirements may change over time, but the Contract does *not* change over time.]

- **Safety**: What emotional and financial safeguards are you going to put in place for the slave, both during the relationship and upon demise of the relationship (or upon the untimely death of the Owner or the slave).

- **Emotional Support and Affirmation:** When you start reviewing slave contracts, you will be struck with all the language giving you, as Master, permission to punish and control the slave. In my experience, a person on the path of *Internal Enslavement* (IE), or *Total Power Exchange* (TPE), is incredibly compliant to begin with. My experience is that the person seeking to serve a Master is much more interested in being recognized and cherished for doing a good job, than for being punished for minor lapses in service.

- **Sexuality**: To whom, and when and how, is the slave to be available? Here, discuss any issues of poly-amory, swinging, multiple slaves, and so forth.

- **Openness**: Is the nature of the relationship to be discreet, or open and obvious to the public, work colleagues, family, etc.?

- **Biological Family:** What provisions are made for any biological family members, especially minor children or aged parents?

- **Discipline**: The nature and extent of control, and

There is no such thing as a "cookie cutter" contract for this kind of relationship. You have to tailor this – or any other preexisting contract – to your own situation. These contracts are only included as examples, not as models.

---

the means (if restricted in any way), for the Owner to enforce the control. Here, discuss any restrictions on specific kinds of discipline. For example, you may wish not to use any type of BDSM implement that is also used for scening. The issue is that implements

---

Note #1: This is in a form that I have actually used. Still, you would have to modify it for your particular circumstances.

Note #2: As this contract was drawn for a female slave, I have left gender references in the feminine.

---

used for scening carry positive associations and related positive emotions. If you start using the same implement for punishment, you will lose some/most/all of those special and positive associations with that implement.

- **Finance**: Explain how pre-existing wealth, as well as income subsequent to the contract, are to be handled. For example, during the training contract, you may not wish to address any aspect of your slave's finances. On the other hand, if your slave candidate is very experienced (has lived as a slave for many years), he/she may expect to surrender personal control over his/her finances.

- **Duration**: How long is your contract? This is a hotly discussed topic. In the gay community, there is a tendency to spend some time getting to know one another before extending a contract without a termination date – a contract for life. Among the heterosexual M/s movement, there is a much stronger tendency to create a series of staged contracts that carry termination dates. There is a substantial camp that believes that a contract must have a termination date in order to be realistic. There is another substantial camp who want their contracts to have termination dates because they recognize that the slave (and even the Master) will change a great deal during this experience, and Master wants to be able to reevaluate the slave every year or so, in light of their experiences together.

Before providing examples of contracts, a note:

EXAMPLE OF A TRAINING CONTRACT

Dated: _____

Preamble

This Contract is between_____, hereinafter referred to as Master, and _____,
hereinafter referred to as *the slave*.

*(Because this contract was initially developed when a new per-
son wanted to explore a relationship with me, but was uncertain
how she would fit in to our established Family, this next line was
included in this actual contract:* This Contract is offered directly
between _____ and _____, and
lives outside the Leather Family structure to which
_____ and _____
are already parties.)*

Caveat

This contract is not legally binding, and is meant only as an aid
better to understand the needs, duties and responsibilities of
_____ and _____
as they begin a period of slave training.

Commitment and Termination

I, _____, hereinafter
referred to as *the slave*, do of my own free will, and being of
sound mind and body, hereby offer myself in consensual training to _____, hereinafter
referred to as Master, for the period beginning _____
_____ and ending on _____,
unless extended or terminated in writing at a different date.

Either party may terminate this Contract at any time before the above named date in the event of a material breach (a material breach is a violation of any contract terms and conditions such that the other party feels his/her benefits under this contract have been destroyed). This Contract may be reviewed, renegotiated, rewritten, or terminated by Master prior to its termination date.

Mutual Respect
This contract describes the respective roles and responsibilities of Master and slave. This contract assumes that each party holds the other in equal respect; that Master and slave each think of the other as having equal value to themselves. Master is not *better* than the slave; the slave is not *less than* the Master.

Contract Provisions
1. To the best of this slave's ability, this slave pledges to honor the terms and the spirit of this Contract, and to study to develop the skills and knowledge necessary to serve Master's wishes and desires. This service will be without ego, pride, or expectations. From this day until the termination or extension of this Contract, this slave pledges at all times to obey Master with humility and to subvert the slave's will and desires to his will and desires. To the extent possible, this slave will hide nothing from Master and answer all questions fully and honestly.

2. During this training period, the slave agrees to obey Master to the best of her ability and to devote herself entirely to Master's pleasure, whether through readings, writings, dress, personal service, or sexual service. This slave also renounces all rights to her own pleasure, comfort, or gratification, except insofar as permitted by Master. The slave agrees to learn what interests and excites Master through exploration and

communication, and to incorporate such discoveries into this relationship.

3. Master now accepts conditional responsibility for this slave. At this stage, this includes the slave's spiritual, social, emotional, physical, and mental well-being. This slave accepts full responsibility for informing Master of all fears, concerns and anxieties on any and all topics, and also to inform him of any real or perceived dangers or safety concerns, whether or not they relate directly to him or to them as a couple. Concurrently, this slave recognizes and agrees that Master's decisions on any topic represent the final word regarding the resolutions of such issues. The slave will not be punished for respectfully stating these concerns. Master strives to listen to the slave's concerns with a clear and open heart and mind.

4. At this time, Master specifically declines to accept responsibility for the slave's financial well-being. This topic will be discussed and addressed in a later contract phase.

5. The slave agrees to dress in the styles and fashions selected by Master, and Master does not make such dress requirements of this slave as to represent financial hardship or burden.

6. During this trial period, Master and slave will play by SSC rather than RACK rules. That is, the slave agrees to accept responsibility for using safewords or safe gestures when necessary. The slave acknowledges that the *physical play* safeword is **red**. Master accepts the responsibility for stopping activities in progress to assess situations where the slave uses a safeword, and he will, to the best of his ability, immediately modify or stop the activity. The slave agrees to hold no ill will due to his decision. Master will not punish the slave for the use of a safeword or safe gesture.

7. During this trial period, this slave agrees to use Master's given name, _____, as an emotional safeword. That is, if Master says something that violates an emotional boundary with the slave, the slave agrees to communicate emotional hurt to Master by prefacing such comments with his given name.

8. The slave agrees to answer fully and promptly any and all questions asked by Master. This is a **FULL DISCLOSURE** Contract. Further, this slave agrees to **volunteer** any information that Master *should know* regarding this slave's physical, mental, or emotional state. Master will not use this information to harm the slave in any way.

9. The slave has previously stated personal limits in a checklist, and Master will not violate these limits without prior negotiation with and consent by the slave.

10. The slave agrees to address _____ as Master, unless otherwise directed. The slave agrees to abide by such Manual of Protocol as Master ultimately creates. The slave agrees to speak respectfully to him at all times, including times not spent in a scene. Master may address the slave in any way he chooses that is not emotionally abusive.

11. Master will furnish the slave with such token(s) of ownership as he sees fit; the slave agrees to wear such symbol(s) at all times, except when the slave states to do so would be inappropriate or would non-consensually involve others.

12. The slave agrees not to have any sexual encounter other than with Master for the duration of this Contract, except to the extent that Master is aware of and approves such encounters. The slave will not engage in sexual self-pleasuring actions without requesting

specific prior permission from Master.

13. The slave agrees to and understands that minor infractions of this Agreement will be dealt with through *Correction,* and that continued inappropriate behavior or material breach of contract will be Punished by withdrawing attention for a specified period, and/or by administering manageable physical discipline in private. Any Correction or Punishment will end in debriefing and forgiveness.

14. If the slave commits an act that violates the trust that Master has placed in the slave, a third party (selected by Master if not mutually agreed upon) will be chosen to hear the issue and to administer a Consequence.

   • The slave agrees to abide by any Ruling made in such a case.

   • There will be a debriefing and forgiveness that will complete the cycle.

   • Time with this slave-in-training must not take away from established times with members of Master's Leather Family.

Fluid Bonding

Unprotected sexual intimacy is a very special Gift between Master and the slave. Master will provide the slave with a hard-copy of his STD report, and agrees that since that STD report, he has not had unprotected sex with any person outside the Family, and will not have unprotected sex with any other person outside the Family while fluid bonded with this slave.

In a general sense, fluid bonding between Master and this slave will occur once these terms and conditions have been met on both sides:

- Test negative for all STDs in a test taken at an appropriate time after last sexual encounter with another person.

- Agree that ALL future sex partners are pre-negotiated.

- Agree that ALL future sex partners will use condoms during intercourse.

- If there is a lapse by either party when striving to conform to these conditions, the party who has had the lapse will return to this negotiated state by immediately bringing this issue – like any other moral/ethical issue – to the other person's attention.

- In the event of an episode of unprotected sex, there will then be a period of protected sex between this slave and Master sufficient to enable the lapsed person to be retested for STDs and to obtain test results.

Master will...

- Use the slave in any way he so desires, and for any purpose he desires.

- Encourage the slave to explore his/her slave heart.

- Serve as a Guide for the slave in the slave's quest for submission and spiritual connection through BDSM.

- Give the slave Directives and Instructions that may carry beyond their physical time together.

- Provide the slave such tokens of ownership as he chooses.

- Correct inappropriate behavior in whatever manner he chooses. Such correction will end in debriefing and forgiveness.

Accepted, understood and agreed to this _____ day of _____, _____.

_____,
Master

_____,
slave

Witnessed: _____

Dated: _____

EXAMPLE OF A COMPLICATED CONTRACT

Here is an example of a very complicated (but specific) contract, taken from many different sources, both from books and web-sites. Obviously, you will need to negotiate your own limits prior to creating this or any other contract. The bulk of this material came from a public-domain website: http://www.londonfetish-scene.com/wipi/index.php/Contract. I sense that it's been cre-ated by an attorney with OCD, but that's strictly my opinion.

*[**Commentary on this Contract**: I hasten to add that I have not ever tried to use this contract – nor would I. I have read it care-fully a number of times and have done some editing, but it does **not**, in fact, sing to me. For a long-term contract, it seems to me that the Master has allowed the slave to retain far too much personal will. Worse, as I read some of these clauses, it would be easy for the slave to trigger a safe period when – in reality – Master is simply training the slave in a way that the slave finds uncomfortable. At any rate, I'll leave it in this book because it is so thorough, and because it should cause you to think about clauses you would want to modify when you create your own specific M/s contract.]*

Dated: _____

Preamble
This Contract is between_____,
hereinafter referred to as Master, and _____,
hereinafter referred to as *the slave*.

Caveat
This contract is not legally binding, and is meant only as an aid
better to understand the needs, duties, and responsibilities of
_____ and _____
as they begin a period of slave training.

Commitment and Termination
I, _____, hereinafter
referred to as *the slave*, do of my own free will, and being of
sound mind and body, hereby offer myself in consensual training to _____, hereinafter
referred to as Master, for the period beginning _____
_____ and ending on _____,
unless extended or terminated in writing at a different date.

Either party may terminate this Contract at any time before the
above named date only in the event of a material breach. Prior
to _____, this Contract will be reviewed,
renegotiated, rewritten, or terminated.

Mutual Respect
This contract describes the respective roles and responsibilities
of Master and slave. This contract assumes that each party
holds the other in equal respect; that Master and slave each think
of the other as having equal value to themselves. Master is not
better than the slave; the slave is not *less than* the Master.

Contract Provisions

1. I agree to please Master to the best of my ability. I understand and accept that I now exist solely for Master's pleasure, to be trained, disciplined, punished and rewarded if and when Master deems it necessary.

2. My Master has agreed not to inflict any physical harm upon my body that would require the attention of anyone outside of our relationship, and has thoughtfully agreed that no discipline, training, or punishment shall take place if he has consumed any alcohol or any drug which would thus impair his ability to keep me from any physical, mental, or emotional harm.

3. My Master and I understand and agree that during the period of this Contract, I hold veto power over any command given by Master only under these specific circumstances:

    a. Where a command conflicts with any existing laws and may lead to fines, arrest, or prosecution.

    b. Where said command may cause extreme damage to my life, such as losing my job, causing family stress, etc.

    c. Where said command may cause long-term bodily harm or psychological trauma.

    d. Where said command is issued in a public place that was not agreed upon beforehand, and reveals to anyone else our relationship.

    e. Where said command is issued during a time that Master has consumed sufficient drugs or alcohol to be considered legally under the influence of said drugs or alcohol, thus impaired in his ability to keep me from harm.

4. I agree to accept, without hesitation, any punishment, reward, discipline, or training regimen my Master decides is needed, whether earned or not, whether physical or mental or emotional.

5. My Master and I have agreed beforehand that punishment, discipline, and/or training, shall not involve any of the following, defined hereby as "Abuse:"

   a. Drawing or release of blood.

   b. Burning or mutilating my body in any way.

   c. Drastic loss of circulation.

   d. Inappropriate and hurtful language intended to upset me (emotional or verbal abuse).

   e. Internal bleeding or complications.

   f. Loss of consciousness, hearing, sight, smell, touch or taste.

   g. Withholding of any necessary materials, such as food, water, sunlight, and/or warmth, for extended periods of time.

   h. Forcing the consumption of any illegal drug in any form at any time.

6. My Master and I have also agreed that because my body now belongs to Master, he shall immediately undertake the responsibility of protecting my body not only from temporary harm, as stated directly above, but also permanent bodily harm.

7. My Master and I have agreed beforehand that punishment, discipline, and/or training shall not involve any of the following, hereby defined as "Permanent Bodily Harm:"

a. Death.

b. Any damage that involves loss of mobility or function, including broken bones.

c. Any permanent marks on the skin, including scars, burns, or tattoos, unless accepted by the slave.

d. Any loss of hair, unless accepted by the slave.

e. Any piercing of the flesh which leaves a permanent hole, unless accepted by the slave.

f. Any diseases that could result in any of the above results, including sexually transmitted diseases.

8. My Master and I have also agreed that because my mind now belongs to Master, he shall immediately undertake the responsibility of protecting my mind from permanent harm.

9. My Master and I have agreed beforehand that punishment, discipline, and/or training, shall not involve any of the following, hereby defined as "Permanent Mental Harm:"

a. Formal brainwashing or hypnosis sessions, unless expressly agreed upon by the slave, and then only by a third party trained professional.

b. Electric shock to temples or any other mind altering application of force or energy.

c. Any mind altering drugs of any kind.

d. Sleep, food, sunlight, or other forms of deprivation or neglect specifically designed to break down my mental capacity in any way.

10. I am aware that as a slave, I will be required to maintain a positive outlook and have *correct thinking,* as such. I

welcome Master's assistance in those areas.

11. My Master and I have agreed that at any time I may utilize a "Safe Word," and that whatever punishment, discipline, or training that is happening at that time shall immediately, and without hesitation, cease, and that time shall be called a "Safe Period," wherein the following rules shall apply:

    a. During any Safe Period, Master and I shall resolve any issues before continuing any punishment, discipline or training.

    b. I must have a valid reason for using a Safe Word, and I must supply a specific reason each time I use it.

    c. No punishments, discipline, or training will take place during a Safe Period, and I shall be free to express my concerns and to speak freely without fear of harm or punishment.

    d. I understand, and willingly accept, that I will continue to address Master with respect and love at all times, and that deviations from this rule are subject to punishment at a later time.

    e. There is no limit to the number of times during any given period the Safe Word may be utilized, and thusly, Safe Periods.

12. My Master and I have agreed that I may ask for a "Free Period" to express my concerns, and to speak freely without fear of harm or punishment. The following rules shall apply at all times:

    a. These shall occur only once per day, and only if requested by Master or I.

    b. They shall never last more than one hour, unless Master wishes it to continue past that time.

    c. They are not cumulative.

    d. My Master has complete control over when these Free Periods shall take place, but has agreed that they shall take place on the same day that I request it.

e. There will be no punishment, discipline or training applied during Free Periods.

13. I understand, and willingly accept, however, that I will continue to address Master with respect and love at all times, and that deviations from this rule are subject to punishment at a later time.

14. For clarification purposes only, the *Safe Period* is a time that all interactions with Master cease immediately while we work to resolve some problem or issue. A *Free Period* is a time that Master grants during which time I am free to choose my own actions/activities; no instruction or training is scheduled during my Free Period.

15. During the duration of this contract, I accept and agree not to take any other Master, Dom or lover, or to be sexual or submissive to any other person, without the express and explicit direction and command of Master. I further understand that to do so without such explicit direction will result in the immediate termination of this contract.

16. My Master has agreed that he shall take no other submissive or slave without first discussing it with me and considering my emotional response to such a proposal.

17. My Master has agreed that he will not upset my emotional balance or ignore me in favor of another submissive or slave.

18. My Master and I have agreed that he shall never under any circumstances give me to another Master, unless the safety guidelines of this contract are wholeheartedly followed by that Master at all times and without exception. It is Master's sole responsibility to determine if this other Master will agree to these terms and will follow these rules.

Master agrees that a breach of contract by any other Master would also be considered by me to be a breach of contract by my Master as well.

19. My Master and I have agreed that all physical evidence of my slavery to Master shall be kept in strictest secrecy, except where Master and I have agreed otherwise.

20. My Master and I have agreed that any alterations to this contract will be printed and signed and attached as addendum to this original contract before said addendum is enforced, and that it will not be necessary to include any edicts or commands or rules, etc., put forth by my Master into this contract.

21. I agree to give all of my worldly possessions to my Master, to give my physical body to my Master, completely and without exception, and to pleasure Master as he requests, and as often as he requests.

22. I understand and accept willingly that Master may punish me, command me, train me, and love me how Master sees fit, at any time, any place, under any circumstance.

23. My Master and I have agreed that Private Rules of Conduct (protocols) shall be created, and that it will be my responsibility always to know any changes to any rules of conduct set forth, and to follow them explicitly without exception; that Master may change these rules of conduct at any time, without prior notice, and that these rules are to govern my actions within and outside the confines of Master's house.

24. My Master and I have agreed that publicly, we shall both conduct ourselves in such a manner as not to call attention to our Master/slave relationship, that I will defer to Master at all times in public, and shall call him by his proper name when appropriate, and that Master has agreed that only

people we have both agreed upon shall know about our relationship and/or contract.

25. Parties or gatherings specifically created for other Masters and slaves shall not be considered public places. Our participation in such parties will be voluntary to both parties. During these gatherings I shall abide by all rules, edicts, and commands of my Master, just as if we were in private, with no exceptions.

26. If, during a party or gathering specifically created for other Masters and slaves, Master wishes me to participate in any way with another slave or Master, he has graciously agreed to discuss this with me beforehand and make such requests in these situations with my acceptance beforehand.

27. I agree and willingly accept my duties as slave.

28. I shall speak of Master in terms of love, respect, and adoration at all times. I will address him at all times as "Sir" or "Master," or however else he sees fit, and I shall abide by all items set forth in this contract, as well as any future edicts, commands or orders to the best of my ability, and understand that there may be adverse consequences should I not carry out Master's requests or follow his rules to his satisfaction.

29. Master has granted me the freedom to to engage in any and all activities not actively forbidden by this contract, or by later edict of my Master, and all rights and privileges not otherwise noted in this contract belong to Master, and he may exercise them as he chooses.

30. Master and I have agreed that no part of this contract is intended to interfere with my career. My Master wishes me to work hard and honestly, in general, and to conduct myself in a manner calculated to bring honor and respect

to both of us.

31. Master has graciously agreed, during periods of work, that I am permitted to schedule appointments, to dress in a manner appropriate to work, and to leave the house when necessary for work. During periods of work, or if at home, I may answer the telephone, if necessary, and discuss business without the express permission of my Master.

32. My Master and I have agreed that for these reasons only, do I have the right to terminate this contract immediately, and with no recourse to myself:

    a. Abuse, as outlined above in section 5a-g, either intentional or accidental, or as a direct result from consuming alcohol or drugs.

    b. Permanent bodily harm, either intentional or accidental, or as a direct result from consuming alcohol or drugs, as outlined above in section 7a-f.

    c. Permanent mental harm, either intentional or accidental, or as a direct result from consuming alcohol or drugs, as outlined above in section 9a-d.

    d. Breach of this contract by another Master, by charge of my Master, or as a direct result from consuming alcohol or drugs, as outlined above in section 18.

    e. Exposed evidence of my slavery as outlined above in section 19.

    f. Any addendums further agreed upon by Master and I that are attached to this contract and signed by both parties will be considered as part of this contract as well.

33. Should any situations occur as outlined in section 32a-f, and should I still continue to want to uphold this contract in full, Master and I shall put in writing what occurred, as well as my decision to continue this contract, and that will be attached to this contract and signed by both of us, unless Master wishes the contract ended at that time because of said situation.

34. I have read and fully understand this contract, and am entering into this contract under my own free will.

35. I have not been coerced in any way to enter into this contract.

36. By signing below, I agree to accept and obey all preceding rules without question, as well as any rules Master may choose to issue at a later date, and I gratefully and willingly consign my body, mind, soul, and worldly possesions to Master, for His pleasure and use any way he sees fit.

I humbly request his acceptance of this contract in full.

Slave:_____ Date: _____

I have read and fully understand this contract in its entirety. I agree to accept this slave as my property, including the slave's body, mind, soul, and worldly possessions, and to care for this slave to the best of my ability. I shall provide for the slave's security and well-being, and command, train, reward and punish the slave, soberly, and as I see fit. I understand the responsibility implicit in this arrangement, and agree that no harm shall ever come to my slave as long as this slave is mine, and this contract is in effect.

I accept my slave's desire to serve me more fully, and take responsibility for the slave's well-being, training, and discipline, to more perfectly serve my will.

Master:_____ Date: _____

I hereby witness this contract, that both parties have entered into such contract willingly and lovingly, and free of coercion or fear.

Witness:_____ Date:_____

EXAMPLE OF AN OWNER'S CONTRACT

[After partners have been together in a structured M/s relation-ship for some time, have grown to trust one another, and are very experienced in BDSM play practices, a simplified contract may work better. This is my current contract with my slave.]

This contract between _____,

the Owner, hereinafter, Master, and _____,

the slave, is as follows:

Contract Provisions

The slave pledges to obey and to serve Master in all ways and at all times, forfeitting all claim to personal time or possessions.

Master pledges to care for and to protect the slave's physical, social, emotional, spiritual, and financial well-being from this point forward in time.

Master: _____ Date _____

slave: _____ Date _____

Witnessed: _____ Date _____

Collars

Collars are usually – but not always – associated with contracts. They are the visible symbol of a power exchange dynamic.

Collars have varying degrees of significance for people in the BDSM community. By wearing a collar, a person may wish to make it known that he or she is submissive. Wearing a collar may similarly be a signal to others that the submissive is "owned" by – or is in a relationship with – a Dominant. It may also be a tangible symbol of the relationship, itself. A lockable collar may further symbolize the transfer of power from the submissive to the Dominant holding the key.

A person wearing a collar to symbolize their relationship with another is said to be **collared**. Some people conduct formal *collaring ceremonies* that are regarded as effectively solemnizing their relationship in the same way as a marriage ceremony.

As a fashion accessory, collars are becoming more common, but not sufficiently so that they would go unnoticed, particularly when worn by men. Many choose to wear their collars only when in private with their partners or with other members of the BDSM community. As BDSM practices move increasingly into middle class society, the role of the collar is also changing. Sometimes, couples who also practice 24/7 M/s and D/s relationships adopt collars that can be mistaken as ordinary chokers or jewelry necklaces that can be worn discreetly in public.

My sense is that formal stages of collaring are seen much more outside than inside the Leather culture. While individuals may name their collars – and the meaning behind their collars – differently, the general sequence goes like this:

- The *collar of consideration* is the first stage and is roughly analogous to a pre-engagement ring. This collar can be removed by the submissive at any time with no ill will, and the relationship would be ended.

- Next comes the ***training collar,*** roughly analogous to an engagement ring; it indicates a deepening relationship in which the submissive is being prepared by the Dominant to serve to the standards the Dominant wishes. Again, the submissive may ask to be released, but the break is considered to be more serious and painful for both parties.

- Finally, the ***full slave collar*** is analogous to a wedding band, and at this point, the submissive is considered to be a formal slave, owned by the Master or Dominant. In the Leather community, this stage is considered permanent. This bond would only be broken if the submissive is released by the Dominant for some exceptional reason. Simple failure of service is not adequate grounds for release, since that would show *control failure* on Master's part, as well as *performance failure* on the slave's part. As with engagement and wedding rings, there are traditions with collars in regard to materials and colors that are appropriate to each level, and they usually become more elaborate as the stages progress.

Personally, I gave my slave a *training collar* before I gave her a *collar of consideration.* My view was that I wanted to assess her acclimatization to the lifestyle (she was fresh from the Land of Vanillas) before I became too heavily invested. For these purposes, I reversed the significance of the collars. That is, she was free to terminate the *training* phase of our relationship, but once she possessed the *collar of consideration,* it was like being engaged.

House collars *(**collars of protection**)* are sometimes used to indicate to others in clubs, homes, and in organizations that provide social spaces that the submissive is under the protection of your House and is to be approached with respect. I have seen protection collars used for submissives who are not yet ready to make their own choices and need time to learn.

Recently, there has been a trend for established, but currently unattached slaves, to petition an established Master for protection (referred to as *wardship*). Once granted, the slave is then said to be a ward of Master XYZ, who is serving as Guardian Master. slave david stein, ward of Master Steve Sampson, prepared an outstanding talk on this issue – presented at the Northeast Master/slave Conference in July, 2006. Currently, our House has extended "wardship" to an unattached "slave-in-waiting," as she seeks a permanent Master. She wears our House collar when at public functions.

Chapter Summary

Here, I began with a preamble about contract theory – why do it. Next, I suggested some basic styles of contracts – simple, time-controlled, and staged. From there, it was an easy step to describing some of the more common elements of M/s contracts – then on to providing some examples of contracts. The chapter ended with a brief review of collars and at least my best shot at explaining their meaning and purpose.

Part VIII: Maintaining a Relationship

Gosh, what hubris! How can I write a section like this? There are books, books, books and experts, experts, experts who really know how this works.

Let me draw attention to the section title for a minute. I could have called this section: "Maintaining a Master/slave Relationship." I didn't, because I've included general truths here. In this section, I'm going to give you some of the lists and quotes that have shaped my life. In some cases, I'll add *commentary.* In my own life, I've been blessed with very long-term relationships. They have ended because I changed – I reinvented myself, and my spouses chose not to follow. Which I respect. I'm still very, very close with them.

I'll start this list with one I picked up recently in a presentation on Master/slave relations. I think it is particularly good. And, I hope you can benefit from the other bits of wisdom as much as I have over the years.

Seven Secrets of Maintaining a Long-Term 24/7 M/s Relationship
Taken from their presentation handout, Master Kurt and slave john have written:
1. Affirm strong, ongoing commitment by both partners to the M/s lifestyle.
2. Remain flexible in negotiating terms of the partnership.
3. Integrate dominance (control) and submission (service) dynamics into everyday activities.

4. Engage in ongoing sexual/BDSM activities that bond partners to one another while reinforcing their self-identities.

5. Recognize that both partners must share common values and interests outside of the M/s lifestyle to maintain a long-term union.

6. Maintain transparent communication between partners.

7. Periodically reset/recalibrate the relationship to ensure that partners remain interested in and connected to one another.

What a great list! Their presentation is outstanding, and I urge you to attend it if you ever have the opportunity.

Watch your Thoughts...

By Frank Outlaw

- Watch your thoughts, they become words.
- Watch your words, they become actions.
- Watch your actions, they become habits.
- Watch your habits, they become character.
- Watch your character, it becomes your destiny.

Commentary: In my view, these are some of life's core truths. Once I realized this, I became very concerned about words and word use. I care a great deal about the connotation of words and closely attend to the words my slave uses. I can "read" quite a bit about my slave's thinking by listening closely to word choice – particularly when the slave is upset.

Another Core Truth

To look is one thing.
To see what you look at is another.
To understand what you see is a third.
To learn from what you understand is still something else.
But to act on what you learn is all that really matters.

Taoist saying

> ***Commentary:*** *Another key to personal Mastery. Not only must one be* **present***, but the person must be* **awake***, aware and have the background experience to* understand *what is happening and to* learn *from it. All this, just to get to the point where one's* action *makes a difference in one's life. This leads us to the next insight.*

Four Stages of Awareness

Often referenced as "The Four Stages of Learning," these concepts appear to have been developed by Noel Burch in the late 1960s. See also: Johari Window.

- Unconscious incompetence: you don't know that you can't do it.
- Conscious incompetence: you know you can't do it.
- Conscious competence: you know you know how to do it.
- Unconscious competence: what you do perfectly is so automatic that you no longer think about it.

Visible and Invisible knowledge: I consider this topic to be **extremely important** when two people are working together – particularly if one person is asking the other to *do something* or to *get something*. YOU know some things that your slave does **not** know. Your slave knows some things that **YOU** don't know. Some knowledge that one or the other of you would consider *very common,* is utterly invisible to the other person. It is useful to be aware that each of you possess knowledge that is *invisible* to your partner. Some examples:

- If you're used to doing your own plumbing, you'll get this right away: you're under the sink working on a repair. You've got your pipe wrenches, but you've forgotten your gunk (or calking tape). You ask your slave to run to the garage and to bring you a tube of calking compound plus a 2" crescent wrench. Nothing. Blank stare. You might as well have tried speaking in Greek. A 2" crescent wrench and calking tape is invisible knowledge to the slave.

- If you're used to doing your own shopping, you'll get this right away: you gave Master something to pick up at the grocery store (go with me on this one – he wanted to go to the store anyway). You say: "Master, when you go out for the wine, would you please bring back a nice steak for our dinner." He comes back with a *choice ribeye.* You blanch: this was to be a special dinner; he knew this. You'd been talking about the candles on the table and the type of Cabernet that was needed – you *assumed* he knew to buy a **prime NY strip steak** – you *assumed he knew* that you ONLY buy prime NY strip steak for this kind of dinner. When you delicately ask Master about it, he explains that it was the right *shape* for the steaks you always buy. Disconnect; invisible knowledge. The *cut* of the meat didn't mean anything – only the *shape* of the meat. He didn't know that ribeye and NY strip look the same. Invisible knowledge to the Master.

Not only are there many areas that are blind from one gender to another – having something to do with how boys and girls are socialized – but also there are knowledge and experience gaps between social classes. For example, if you're in a truck stop, *chatting with the waitress* is perfectly normal. Ditto if you're at TGIFriday's. The waitperson is likely to be chatty as a way of making larger tips. Not a problem. However, if you're in an elite restaurant with linen service and you start speaking with the professional waitperson, you immediately telegraph that you're clueless about social etiquette. In this case, conversing with the wait staff is improper, and your host is going to draw many unflattering inferences about you from that gaffe.

Coming around very gingerly to the topic of *social etiquette,* and *visible and invisible knowledge,* and *unconscious incompetence*, I'll give you a concrete example that ties back to slave training. Depending upon the person's upbringing – gender won't matter, here – some people bend at the waist when bending over in a kitchen (or elsewhere) to remove something from a low storage cabinet. Those with a more careful upbringing will squat – in order that their rear-ends not stick out. This degree of personal behavior is invisible to most people and will telegraph your upbringing.

The message, then, is that in forming a new relationship, the Master must be extremely sensitive to different sets of assumptions between Master and slave. The slave may be working as hard as he/she can and still seem to be *missing* important points that the Master thinks are perfectly obvious.

> ***Commentary:*** *In training a slave, much of your responsibility is to walk him/her through these stages. Personally, I have frequently reflected on these four stages of awareness when considering an aspect of my slave's action that requires more attention. Even more than that, as a Master, you must be able to distinguish between visible and invisible knowledge.*

Communication

What a complex topic. I don't want to start down the path of teaching communication skills in a book on M/s relations, but you might consider some of these questions/issues and build strengths where you sense they may need building.

- What evidence do you have that you are able to communicate clearly, confidently, and persuasively? In your work life, are you looked upon as a particularly clear communicator?

- Do your ideas have selling power? Is it your experience that people follow your ideas?

- Have you taken courses in effective communications?

- When you speak, do you use simple words, short sentences, and clear word-pictures?

- When your slave describes his/her unique situation, do you take the time to listen attentively and to respond so your slave feels acknowledged and respected? (Unique *situation* can mean a shopping experience. Does the person with whom you are speaking feel valued and validated?)

Commentary: I distinguish between talking and speaking. One "talks to" someone or "speaks with" someone. In my view, talking is one-way. Talking is lecturing.

Upsets

How do you reconnect with your slave after an upset? What if it's YOU who became upset and the slave was not at fault? Or, what if the slave WAS at fault and caused the upset? I've already covered *talking sticks* as our Family's way of working through upsets. I would say that the talking sticks are the second level of response. My first level of response to an upset slave is to revert *immediately* to a higher level of protocol. If she's had an upset and spoken curtly to me, I might lightly ask: "Do I take it that the answer was 'Sir, with respect, Sir, **only** if it pleases you, Sir.'?" (For those of you who have not read my Protocols book, or who are not familiar with forms of address in a Leather M/s relationship, that sentence means "No, I won't do it unless you absolutely require it of me.")

But, this last paragraph carries a very important hidden concept. Notice the way I described my slave's frame of mind. I said that she "had an upset" as opposed to "was upset." This is not trivial: if you are *being* upset, then you are *coming from your being* – your inner self – and your whole being is about *upset.* I don't want to give it that weight, so I refer to it as *having an upset.* That way, you can think about either *having* or *not having* the upset – you can come from choice – not from *effect.* (Yes, I'm an *est* graduate. Also Landmark Education. My slave has also gone through a number of the Landmark offerings.) However, sometimes, for whatever reason, the Master's emotions may cause a problem and the slave may have to defuse the situation. Therefore, it's important that BOTH parties have some conflict resolution skills. [There is quite a bit Internet material on this; you may wish to start with www.crnhq.org and click on "12 Skills Summery."]

Goal Setting

- Are you clear about what you want to achieve in your life?
- Look back at your life and examine where you started and measure how far you've come.
- Are you satisfied with where you are today?
- Are you excited and enthusiastic about your goals?

Commentary: Have you ever sat down with your slave and had a business meeting? A meeting where you discuss your personal goals for the next M-months or Y-years? A meeting where you explain the skills you wish to master to accomplish your goals; a meeting where you list proposed activities that support the skills, and so forth? Depending upon your degree of experience with **planning-feedback loops,** *you could build in periodic evaluation points that would enable you to adjust and correct your timeline or activities as you proceed in your plan. Does this sound a bit otherworldly? Let me point out: life is really short. If you don't plan your work and work your plan, you'll wake up much older with little to show for the time you spent on earth. Please see the section in the next chapter entitled "Plan your Future" for a step-by-step description about how to accomplish this kind of planning.*

Balancing Priorities

- Do you find yourself handling the same piece of paper over and over? Do you organize your life to get the most done in the least amount of time? (www.pilesto-files.com click on "special reports.")

- Do you put off burdensome tasks or do you find that your "to-do list" keeps growing longer? Are you able to prioritize your life to maximize growth and achievement?

- Do you make time with your slave to discuss your career challenges and problems within your biological family?

- Do you take time out to release stress and free yourself from everyday worries and anxieties?

- Do you have adequate help at home? Are you over-taxing one slave? (Just ask, your slave will tell you.)

Ongoing Improvement

How do you grow, personally? How do you add skills? Do you expect your slave to grow in this M/s relationship? Will you be satisfied if your slave has the same skills in five years that he/she has right now?

- Are you living your life based on a philosophy of ongoing improvement?

- Do you feel that your greatest achievements are still ahead of you? Do you remain curious about the world around you?

- Do you have a methodology for living up to the best that is within you?

- After a period of rejuvenation following a substantial success, do you challenge yourself to continue to reach even greater levels of success?

- Do you expect, encourage, and enable ongoing improvement from those within your family?

Taking Risks

- Are you willing to create new opportunities by taking risks? In what area are you willing (or unwilling) to take risks? Financial risks; emotional risks; relationship risks; social risks; workplace risks?

- Are your convictions more important to you than your need for approval from authority figures?

- When you are going out on a limb, do you trust your abilities?

- Do you allow enough preparation time when you set out to create the best opportunity for yourself? Do you ever prepare a "briefing book" or go through a "trial run" when preparing to propose a new idea either to your slave, or in a work or social setting? These are certainly standard business practices (at least in successful businesses), so why not bring them into your Household?

- Are you aware that it is often riskier *not to do anything* than to make a bold move? In the business world, this is referred to as *"lost opportunity risk."*

Responsibility

- As Head of Family, do you step out of the way and enable your Family members to assume a greater share of responsibility?

- Does your slave strive to take a greater amount of initiative?

- Do you encourage your Family members to become independent from your daily direction?

- Do you reward your Family members who take on greater responsibility? (Personal note: we often dress in military fetish for dinners. I have begun to award military ribbons to recognize outstanding service.)

Motivation

- When you are having a very bad day, do you consciously take action and deal with the problem head on? Clearly, your slave needs to know whether or not your *upset* is a Family matter.

- When you find that your slave hasn't followed what you *thought* was a clear Directive, do you try to turn the negative experience into a learning lesson for further growth? Hint: if you gave your slave a clear Directive and the slave apparently ignored it, chances are, one of two things just occurred. First, you were not nearly as clear as you thought you were about your Directive; second, your Directive may not have been as good an idea as you thought and your slave has outthought you on this score and self-corrected. Tread carefully, lest you create an automaton, rather than a forward-thinking slave. (No, I didn't miss the problem of *willfulness* in the second part of the discussion – and I'm glad you caught it, too. M/s relationships can be tricky.)

Rules of the Mind

- What you expect to happen tends to happen. (This is a cousin to one of my favorite expressions: *You get what you resist.* The common denominator is that when you dwell on something a great deal – whether positive or negative – you tend to notice it when it finally comes to pass. Also, when you expect to one thing to happen you limit your own ability to consider and act on creative alternatives.)

- Imagination is more powerful than knowledge; your body will produce what your mind believes. (In many cases, you don't notice something until you realize that the *something* can possibly exist. That is, until you hold a concept of something, you may find that it's right in front of you, but you don't recognize it for what it is. This phenomenon gave rise to the bumper sticker you sometimes see: *Some things have to be believed to be seen.*)

- Every thought or emotion has a physical reaction. (This concept is at the root of the observation from the field of psychology that there is no distinction to a person between something that is *real* and something that is *imagined.*)

- A belief programmed into the subconscious mind will remain until it is replaced by another idea; your mind seeks validation for previous beliefs. (This is another important concept not only for understanding how you think, but also for slave training.)

Twelve things to remember:

Marshal Field (founder of the department store chain)

1. The value of time
2. The success of perseverance
3. The pleasure of working
4. The dignity of simplicity
5. The worth of character
6. The power of kindness
7. The influence of example
8. The obligation of duty
9. The wisdom of economy
10. The virtue of patience
11. The improvement of talent
12. The joy of originating

The Dali Lama's Instructions for Life

As said for the new millennium. But, why not take his words beyond that.

1. Take into account that great love and great achievements involve great risk.

2. When you lose, don't lose the lesson.

3. Follow the three Rs:

   - Respect for self
   - Respect for others and
   - Responsibility for all your actions.

4. Remember that *not getting what you want* is sometimes a wonderful stroke of luck.

5. Learn the rules so you know how to break them properly.

6. Don't let a little dispute injure a great friendship.

7. When you realize you've made a mistake, take immediate steps to correct it.

8. Spend some time alone every day.

9. Open your arms to change, but don't let go of your values.

10. Remember that silence is sometimes the best answer.

11. Live a good, honorable life. Then, when you get older and think back, you'll be able to enjoy it a second time.

12. A loving atmosphere in your home is the foundation for your life.

13. In disagreements with loved ones, deal only with the current situation. Don't bring up the past.

14. Share your knowledge. It's a way to achieve immortality.

15. Be gentle with the earth.

16. Once a year, go someplace you've never been before.

17. Remember that the best relationship is one in which your love for each other exceeds your need for each other.

18. Judge your success by what you had to give up in order to get it.

19. Approach love and cooking with reckless abandon.

Reflections on Life

Collected by Robert J. Rubel

- A commitment is doing what you said you would do long after the feeling you said it in has passed.

- Be bold about ideas, tentative about people.

- You can never solve the problem using the same logic that created it in the first place. (Einstein)

- Vision without action is a daydream. Action without vision is a nightmare.

- There is not a *right* way to do a *wrong* thing. **Knowing** what's right doesn't mean much unless you **do** what's right.

- The one important thing I have learned over the years is the difference between taking one's work seriously and taking one's self seriously. The first is imperative; the second is disastrous.

- Tact is the art of making a point without making an enemy.

- Professionals are people who can do their job when they don't feel like it. Amateurs are people who can't do their job when they DO feel like it.

- If you have tried to do something and failed, you are vastly better off than if you had tried to do nothing and succeeded.

- The average person has about 10,000 ideas per day; the problem is that same "average person" had 99.9% of those same ideas the day before. And the day before, and the day before. Actually, the hidden problem, here, is with overworked ideas.

- Things don't change, we do; there is always a way if you're committed.

- In the long run, it's more orderly to convert chaos to system than to cover chaos with system.

- What you are afraid to do is a clear indicator of the next thing that you need to do.

Commentary: The last few sub-heads – and their associated bullets – are intended to spark your thinking about how to configure your Household. I said from the beginning of this book that my Household is somewhat cerebral. But, we find these ideas to be challenging; they often prompt us to reconsider how we're doing things.

Chapter Summary

Okay, we're coming to the end of the book. In this chapter I've tackled the task of proposing some approaches to maintaining a relationship. Largely, I've included bulleted points that cover a wide range of topics that impinge on the subject of *relationships*. Much of what is included in this chapter requires *reflection* and *introspection*; you have to think about yourself and who you are both as a person, and as a Master. Among other topics, I touched on *communication, goal-setting,* and *risk-taking*. I also touched on *responsibility* and *motivation* within *the M/s structure*. Finally, I brought the chapter to a close with the Dali Lama's *Instructions for Life* and a collection of aphorisms that I have collected over the years.

An M/s Studies Book

Part IX: How's it Going?

In my experience, it takes a lot of work to ensure that a relationship remains healthy, vibrant, and fulfilling for each partner. If you've reached this point in the book and decided that this makes reasonable sense, then here are a few thoughts about maintaining your relationship in tip-top shape. This chapter contains a brief listing of things that have particularly helped my M/s relationship.

Know Your Priorities

As Master Jim Glass says: "Decisions in this relationship always serve the Family's wellbeing." Unlike a Vanilla relationship, a Leather Master/slave structured relationship is serving a *higher purpose.* As Master, it is incumbent upon you to keep that vision in the forefront of your mind and behavior. You have much more to do in this kind of relationship than you would have to do in a husband/wife relationship.

Don't *Drift:* Plan Your Future

In the same way that a Master/slave relationship is based on structure, you may – like me – find it extremely helpful to put more thought and structure into your lives as a couple (or threesome, or more).

As Lewis Carroll said in Alice in Wonderland, "If you have no destination, any road will take you there."

I'm completely committed to thinking through where I want to be in five or ten or twenty years, and then focusing my energies towards that goal. I've found that to be *very* successful. The more clearly I can explain my goals and work through the necessary steps to attain the goals, the more easily my new life unfolds before me. There are many planning models you can use to build a personal/Family plan: pick one and use it. Here is a very basic (and well-established) model that works well for individuals or small businesses that don't have a lot of strategic planning experience:

1. **Identify your purpose (mission statement).** This is the statement (or statements) that describe why your Family exists, i.e., its basic purpose. What are you and your slave all about? Are you focusing primarily on yourselves and your relationship, or are you intending to give something back to the Community? If you intend to give back, what are you giving back? Time? Service? Money? Wisdom? The statements will change somewhat over the years.

2. **Select the goals your Family must reach to accomplish its mission.** Goals are general statements about what you need to accomplish to meet your purpose, or mission, and they address major issues/constraints that you will face in the process.

3. **Identify specific approaches or strategies that must be implemented to reach each goal.** Strategies often change quite a bit as the Family eventually conducts more robust strategic planning, particularly by more closely examining what are called the **external** and **internal** environments of the Family. An external environment concerns outside forces that have an impact on your Family. The internal environment concerns itself with how the two (or three or four...) of you have learned to interact and work together.

4. **Identify specific action plans to implement each strategy.** These are the specific job responsibilities that each member must undertake to ensure effective implementation of each strategy. Objectives should be

clearly worded to the extent that people can assess if the objectives have or have not been met. Ideally, each type of job function within the Family would have a work plan, or set of objectives. For example, if one objective is to develop a House Protocols book, that project would have its own action plan. If one objective is to improve the Family's wardrobe, that objective would have its own action plan. Ditto if the objective was to obtain new training in order to obtain a better job in order to bring more money into the Family.

5. **Monitor and update the plan.** Business planners regularly reflect on the extent to which the goals are being met and whether action plans are being implemented. Perhaps the most important indicator of Family success comes from comments by friends who notice positive changes in your life.

Say Nothing – Then Think About It

Menander – one of the rulers of the Indo-Greek Kingdom in northern India from 150 to 130 BCE – is quoted as having said: "*Nothing is more useful than silence.*" I'll second that. It's saved me many times, and I recommend it as an active medication in all M/s relationships. It's closely followed by the admonition that when thinking about saying something, carefully *plan* your key points in light of what you can discern about the way your slave is looking at the situation from his/her viewpoint. That is; study to understand how your slave feels about the situation before you jump in with your interpretation or opinion.

Give Your slave Some Free Time

This relationship is not about getting your shirts cleaned and organizing your shirts in color-order on hangers in your closet. Well... it certainly *can be* about that, too, but it can be more about *connection* and *purpose.* It can be much more about living a purposeful and thoughtful life in which order supports tranquil-ity.

Because there is soooooooooo much to do in life, and in this structured relationship, I find it very hard to release my slave for *free time*. I am often described as *driven.* At age 61, I have an acute sense of how little time there is in life. There are count-less books to read, countless skills to hone or to acquire, and countless places to travel. I have *uses* for a personal assistant in many, many aspects of my life.

It's hard for me to release my slave to do something that doesn't appear to directly support our M/s structure. I often must remind myself that giving this *free time* supports my slave's emotional and physical wellbeing, which in turn, DOES support our M/s structure. Besides, slaves are subject to stress and burnout – especially when juggling career, family responsibilities, social activities, and regular daily activities, **in addition to** serving Master. You can find information concerning signs and symp-toms of burnout on the Internet, but basically, the symptoms may manifest in various areas such as the cognitive, psychological, physical, social, and behavioral. Symptoms can include:
- depression
- irritability
- anxiety
- hyperexcitability
- negativism
- excessive anger
- inability to concentrate and make decisions
- loss of motivation
- physical exhaustion
- headaches
- gastrointestinal distress
- loss of energy
- appetite disturbances
- sleep disorders

- increased interpersonal conflicts
- decrease in social activities

So: be sure to release your slave periodically.

Catch Your slave *Doing Right* – Demonstrate Your Appreciation

Often, people only comment when their partner does something wrong. I believe that there is serious risk in this. If you are always catching the person making a mistake, then your slave is likely to start to anticipate that whenever you offer a comment – even a neutral or positive comment – you're hiding what you are *really* thinking. Clearly, this reaction is the opposite of what you want or need.

So, to break that possible cycle, I leave little *congratulatory notes* around for my slave. *Good Job: The bathroom is spotless. Thank you.* Sometimes, I will go up to my slave and remark on what a competent job is being done on some chore or another.

And, I'm careful about taking her out to dinner occasionally – considering the tremendous amount of work my slave puts into our formal dinners.

Oh yes, and I make sure that there are flowers throughout the house. Every week.

Learn to *Focus/Refocus* Your slave

Sometimes my slave *drifts*. My slave forgets and drifts back to actions or speech from the Vanilla world. Serving dinner, the slave jumps up from Table to bring something. First, how did that *something* get forgotten? Second, since we are already at Table, the slave must ask permission to get up. What to do, what to do, what to do??? The slave is serving from the heart; this is good. The slave is anticipating a need and moving to meet it; this is good. But this action, jumping up from table to bring something without first asking permission, is devoid of protocol; this is *not* good. It doesn't fit our structured relationship and deserves Attention.

In my world, if my slave jumps up from Table to get something during one of our formal fetish Dinners, she knows she's "in trouble." One of our Dining Protocols is that she can only walk around the table counter-clockwise. As she sits to my right, that means that she has to walk past me to get back to her chair. This affords the (lovely) opportunity to *correct her* for her impulsive action. Our *punishment* calls for her to bend over, hands spread on the seat of her chair, legs spread wide apart while I…

Ah, but if she *really* drifts – loses focus – but the *drift* is minor, I signal my slave to assume a Full Present position (kneeling, legs apart, hands behind back, head up) and recite this poem. (Thanks to Master Michael Yongue, Head Master, The House of Ptolemy, for sparking this idea.)

Master...
i am your slave; and i reaffirm
that i have given myself to You completely.
Master...
i seek the serenity to serve you effortlessly
with grace and elegance.
Master...
i seek to make your life a magical place, surrounded by beauty.

To deliver these gifts,
i seek understanding of my shortcomings,
i seek patience with my humanity,
i seek emotional love and support.

For i am Your property, Master, to do with as You choose.
For i am Yours,
Forever.

Occasionally, your slave may seem to take leave of his or her senses and experience a more serious drift. In these cases, you can achieve *focus* by taking away something that is important, or by altering a routine.

By way of example: I recently had a problem with my slave, who broke two rules at once – an extremely unusual situation. First, my slave failed to follow a direct written instruction and second, she failed to fully communicate with me about the status of that assigned task. While the details of "the story" are unimportant, the lesson is that *something* had to be done to get us back on the same track. I settled on asking my slave to restate in writing what had happened – from her perspective – and to explain to me why the assignment had not been completed, and how she would deal with it if the situation were reversed and she had a slave who did this.

When I gave this assignment, I was particularly careful not to make my slave feel "wrong." I explained that I was having trouble understanding her *behaviors* in light of our M/s relationship.

Her four-page, single-spaced reply was extremely helpful for both of us. We were able to pinpoint the breakdown (it had to do with some *assumptions* on both our parts, as is often the case) and we agreed to be sensitive to these kinds of situations in the future. We each had to *let go* of our positions about "being right."

So, *focus* means letting go; *focus* means removing preconceived notions about the way things *should be* and replacing them with *how Master wants the slave to act.* Focus is never easy to maintain in the beginning of a structured relationship, but it is well worth it in the long run. (Focus is a major step toward self-mastery, which is very important in this dynamic.)

When Your Relationship Runs into *Trouble*, Revert to Protocols

Protocols reinforce the power exchange dynamic of the relationship and represent a safe harbor during stressful times. There's nothing like having the slave resting in a Full Present position while you work through some issue. If the conversation starts to sound too *chatty,* try asking: "And how would that sound in protocol?"

Don't ask Questions to which You Don't Want Answers

This is a kissing-cousin to the trial attorneys' motto: "Don't ask questions for which you don't already know the answer."

In my experience raising children, there were certain things I simply *didn't want to know.* There were areas where they needed privacy. Similarly, in training my slave, there are certain things I simply don't want to ask about. This is because I either already know that a task/project wasn't done exactly as I would like, or *whether or not it was done my way* is not important enough to give it the significance of a question. When I observed that my slave had done something in *what I would consider* to be an odd way, I often had to fight the urge to stop and ask for an explanation, because if I did ask, I found that my slave would become extremely anxious, as my questions carried a connotation of criticism. In fact, I was merely trying to figure out how my slave *thought* and *worked.*

Learn to Manage Discussions

While Master certainly has the role, responsibility, and authority to *decide,* he/she also has the obligation to *lead.* That means that Master must master the art of leading discussions with his/her slave to produce the desired results – and to avoid allowing the conversation to drift into unproductive areas (areas not supporting the purpose of the discussion). Master may ask the slave many questions about the slave's preferences in a matter, but Master will then fit decisions about those preferences into HIS/HER assessment of overall Family needs.

To facilitate discussions, I like to round out each discussed idea with a 15-20 second position summary. I make a point never to leave a meeting or discussion unless everyone has agreed that the key issues have been addressed to everyone's satisfaction.

Caution: That doesn't mean everyone got what they wanted, it only means that if there is lingering disagreement, everyone has agreed to disagree.

Know what slaves Fear Most

slaves most fear **rejection** and **failure**. In most cases that I know of, slaves have made substantial life adjustments and personal sacrifices to be with their Master. They are *invested* in the relationship. Certainly more than in a vanilla relationship, the slave needs affirmation; the slave needs to know he/she is *doing right and makes a difference in your life.* Consider leaving little *ataboy* notes around. Consider being extra thoughtful.

Chapter Summary

Now we're in a Relationship and the question is: "How're you doing?" I made a series of suggestions: know your priorities, plan your future to avoid *drifting* in the relationship, don't be quick to criticize your slave, give your slave free time to recover from the rigors of the *structured relationship*, and find ways to catch your slave doing things right, not wrong. I went on to suggest some ways that you could refocus your slave and suggested some approaches to take if you feel your relationship is running into trouble. I also urged you not to ask questions of your slave for which you didn't want answers – to learn to tolerate a certain level of ambiguity in the relationship. I also suggested that you learn to manage discussions, rather than to allow them to drift freeform into topics that might be unproductive. At the very end, I pointed out that slaves most fear *rejection* and *failure,* and that it should take very little external control to obtain the goals and objectives your slave has agreed to by virtue of being your slave.

Epilogue

I hope you have enjoyed reading this book as much as I have enjoyed writing it. While living it, I've also been studying this form of structured relationship for a number of years, reading widely in what literature I could find and attending M/s conferences that offered instructive seminars. I have learned a great deal by watching others work through their own relationship issues – and I am constantly striving to find ways to improve my own working relations with my slave.

I am interested in your reactions to this book. Please feel free to contact me. Contact information appears on the last page.

Appendix A

The Safe Call

There is always a first meeting. Even if the two of you have met casually at a kinky event, there will always be a *first time* to meet to discuss possible play. This appendix is about the way you go about setting up that first meeting. And possibly that second meeting.

A safe call is a prearranged agreement with an outside party whose job it is to call the police and/or get help if they don't hear from you by a particular time when you are meeting socially – playing – for the first time with someone you don't know. Often, it is used for second or third meetings as well – or until you feel you know this person reasonably well. This procedure can be used by anyone whether they are new to the BDSM scene or a well-seasoned veteran. There is a place for it even in the Vanilla world. *Whenever you use a safe call, be sure that the person you intend to meet knows that you are using this procedure.* Not only is *deterrence* an important aspect of the safe call, it would be impolite for you to meet someone for the first time and – without letting the person know you're using these procedures – have to say: "Excuse me, I have to make my safe call right now."

Typically, a slave/submissive/bottom sets up the safe call, although a Dom/Master/Top may arrange them as well. Actually, either party can set up their own separate safe calls. You gather enough non-changable personal contact information to be sure that the person can be found, if need be, and deliver it to a third party. You then set a time by which the third party must be contacted. If the call isn't made, then the third party calls the police, tells them that you might have been taken captive, and gives them the pertinent information.

There are a few more details to a safe call. First, the caller typically has a non-obvious phrase or password to indicate that they are safe. This way, even if they end up being held hostage and are forced to make the safe call, they can still alert the third party. Second, the caller lets their prospective date know that a safe call has been arranged. The only thing that the prospective date should know is at what time the call needs to be made. (Be careful, time flies when playing. Set an alarm on your cell phone to remind you.) It should raise a red flag if the prospective date presses for more information and/or tries to dissuade you from setting up the safe call. An ethical person won't mind having a safe call in place – but remember: you must have notified your play partner that you're using safe call procedures. Third, you should plan to arrive in a separate vehicle at least 15 minutes early so that you can park and get to the meeting place before your prospective date. You don't want this person to be able to identify your car or vehicle license number. Similarly, you should watch this person leave the area before you approach your car to depart.

Basic information is:

- Name and physical description of the person
- Drivers license number (you should have your prospective date fax you a copy of the DL – how do you know it is a valid DL number?)
- Phone number where you will be meeting or playing
- Address where you will be meeting and/or playing (Playing is not recommended for the first meeting.)
- Type of location – home, restaurant, etc.
- When the safe call should be made (When meeting and leaving? Every hour on the hour with only five minutes of grace period? etc.)

- A non-obvious phrase to indicate that you are safe (e.g.: "Okay, then put on your pajamas and watch a video, I don't care." Means you're safe.)

- Any pertinent details on the meeting that you have arranged.

Additional safety notes:

- Meet the first time at a restaurant such as IHOP™ that will have multiple cameras scanning the room. If you feel threatened, you can mention these cameras to the person you're meeting.

- The first time you play (or maybe even the first few times you play), avoid doing anything that may leave you unable to escape. This would include bondage activities, getting into anyone else's car, and so forth. You can save that type of fun for a later date.

- In this day of Caller ID, submissives, in particular, may have worries about talking on the phone with a Dom before they're ready to exchange names, addresses, and phone numbers (particularly when they have a listed phone number). If someone gives you a phone number and requests that you call, has Caller ID, and you don't block your phone number from being trans-mitted, he or she may be able to obtain more informa-tion about you than you could believe.

- However, your local phone company may allow you to block the transmission of your phone number to the next phone number (ONLY the next phone number) that you dial. Dialing *67 accomplishes that where I live. Try it out first with someone you trust, or check for the details about how your phone company does this in your local phone book. It may not be available everywhere.

Appendix B

Master/slave Conferences

Over the past few years, weekend conferences have evolved that feature Master/slave relations over BDSM activities. Concurently, there are competitions held at these conferences for Master/slave titles that represent specifiic regions. In order to compete for the International Master/slave title, you first have to win a regional title, then compete again at Southplains Leatherfest in Dallas in February. Here are the related website links.

"Feeder" Conferences

[Note: conferences are listed in order of occurrence after Southplains in February. Thus, the Southwest conference appears last because it occurs in January – at the end of the competition cycle for the previous year.]

- **Northeast** (Washington, D.C., July)
  http://www.mastertaino.com/Master_slave_Conference.htm

- **Great Lakes** (Indianapolis, August)
  http://greatlakesleather.org/web/schedule.html

- **Northwest** (San Jose, CA, TBA)
  [Note, this is a new member of the M/s contest community. Their participation was announced at Southplains in 2006, and, at this writing, their website does not mention the regional conference.)
  http://www.smodyssey.com/main.html

- **Southeast** (Charlotte, N.C., October)
[Note – this event will not be held in 2006; check their website for updates.
http://www.togetherinleather.org
- **Southwest** (Phoenix, January)
http://www.southwestleather.org

Culminating Event

International Master/slave Conference (Dallas, February)
http://www.southplainsleatherfest.com

Important Link

This link will enable you to identify all these websites at one time and also gives the names of current and past titleholders. Excellent historical site.

http://www.togetherinleather.org/MsRegionals.html

About the Author

Dr. Rubel is an educational sociologist and researcher by training.
Immediately after college, he taught
high school English in South-Central
Los Angeles. Returning to graduate
school, he earned an EdM (Boston
University) and PhD (University of
Wisconsin) in the area of crime
prevention in public schools. After
serving a stint as a Visiting Fellow at
the U.S. Department of Justice, he
formed a 501(c)(3) that specialized
in crime prevention in public schools.
He ran that firm for 17 years. During
part of that period, he also was a
founding member of the American Association of Woodturners,
which he also ran for its first three years of existence. In his mid-
40s, Bob decided to change careers utterly and joined a stock
brokerage and future brokerage firm in Washington, DC. Within
six months, he was made a Principal of the futures brokerage
side of the firm and five months later was named CEO. He ran
the company for four years. Upon the request of a close friend,
Dr. Rubel returned to Austin to help this person start a new
company. He worked as the corporate operations officer for five
years, and then retired to pursue his passion as an erotic and
fetish art photographer.

Robert (Bob) Rubel has been involved in the BDSM scene for a
number of years, throwing himself into the literature of the field as
though it were an academic study. He frequently attends BDSM

weekend conferences. Within his local community, Robert (who is also known as "Corwin", the erotic and fetish photographer – www.photosbycorwin.com) has served the BDSM community in the following ways: Board Member of NLA-Austin, Council Member of SAADE (School for Advanced American Dominant Education) and Director of SAADE's Special Interest Group for Master/slave relations. He served for two years as part of the Leadership Core of the Austin Mentors Program where he taught fire play and M/s relations.

Robert's books include:

- Protocols: Handbook for the female slave (2006)
- Protocol Handbook for the Leather slave: Theory and Practice (2006)
- Flames of Passion: Handbook of Erotic Fire Play (2006 with David Walker)
- Squirms, Screams and Squirts: Now you can turn great sex into extraordinary sex (2007)

Three books of erotic and fetish photography:
- Parts: The Erotic Photographic Art of Robert J. Rubel, PhD (2006)
- Wholes: The Erotic Photographic Art of Robert J. Rubel, PhD (2006)
- Holes: The Erotic Photographic Art of Robert J. Rubel, PhD (2006)

To purchase any of these books, or to learn about presentations offered by Dr. Rubel, please see: www.RubelPresents.com. Links on the "Books" page will tie you back to Amazon.

To view Dr. Rubel's erotic and fetish photography, see: www.photosbycorwin.com.

To view Dr. Rubel's nature photography, see: www.scenesofbeauty.com.

To contact Dr. Rubel, use: Robert@RubelPresents.com. In the subject line, say: Book Contact (this will cause your e-mail to bypass the spam filter).

While not a licensed therapist, Dr. Rubel is also available to provide informed guidance about your own M/s relationship. If contacting him for *that* purpose, please put the phrase "M/s Question" in the subject line.

Other Books by Robert Rubel

Academic Books:
The Unruly School: disorders, disruptions and crime. Robert J. Rubel (D.C. Heath and Company: Lexington, Massachusetts) 1977.

Violence and Crime in the Schools. Keith Baker and Robert J. Rubel (eds.) (D.C. Heath and Company: Lexington, Massachusetts) 1980.